# DON'T: A Woman's Word

**Elly Danica**

*gynergy books, 1988*

Copyright, ©, 1988, **Elly Danica**
*Second Printing, November, 1988*
*Third Printing, April, 1989*

Design: Libby Oughton
Typesetting: Pièce de Résistance Ltée
Printing: Les Editions Marquis Ltée

gynergy books
Box 132
Charlottetown, P.E.I.
C1A 7K2 Canada

With thanks to the Canada Council and the
Saskatchewan Arts Board for their support.

The publisher wishes to thank all the women
at WestWord 3 where this manuscript came to
light.

**Canadian Cataloguing in Publication Data**
Danica, Elly, 1947-
Don't : a woman's word
ISBN 0-921881-05-3
I. Title.
PS8557.A65D66 1988     C813'.54     C88-098530-5

*For my Oma in Holland and her daughter, my mother*
*For my sister Laurie (1959-1980)*
*And for all my other little sisters*

# Introduction

The book you are about to read is unlike anything that has ever been written. This is a courageous, exemplary book written by an extraordinary woman, an incest survivor. It is the story of a heroine who moves forward word by word, into her memory and into her story, and who risks it all with every sentence, every image. For, between the book and the writing — that is to say between what is told and how it is told — there is a woman who, with all her being, has chosen to tell the unbearable, has taken it upon herself to break the silence.

When I first read the manuscript, I experienced a range of feelings — from outrage to utter dejection, from anger to the deepest of sadness. It took me several days to finish reading it, because this is a book that is read with a lump in the throat, a tightness in the heart, tears. Reading this book, we bear the child and the woman in ourselves. Reading this book, we share intimately what seems beyond words.

*Don't* is a book that reminds us just how much sexual violence, whatever its form (incest, rape, pornography, flashing, verbal harassment), is not only a repeated assassination of our vitality, our dignity and our creativity, but also a way for men to occupy our lives, in the same way one "occupies" a country. Sexual violence doesn't end with the act. It occupies our thoughts and our time. It imprisons us in a space of fear, a space of shame, a space of self-negation. Sexual violence cuts us off from joy and from all those cheerful landscapes that as children we imagined lasting a lifetime.

*Don't* goes beyond the simple act of recounting, for the lucidity and determination of the author spares us no detail. It brings us to the core of suffering and humiliation. Each word torments beyond anything we could imagine of the violence and terror that batter the child, the young girl, then the adolescent. All in the name of the father and his power to exterminate.

Yes, this book takes us beyond the act of recounting, because the fact that is exists at all attests to the author's resistance, courage, intelligence and love of life. Elly Danica is without a doubt more a fighter than a survivor. She discovered within herself a way to find the thread and the colour of her life. Day after day, she patiently wove her life together until the courage came to speak, and one day, the strength to be able to write:

> *From the secret place. Soul dwelling:*
> *found. Self: found. Heart: found. Life:*
> *found. Wisdom: found. Hope, once lost:*
> *found. Process: never lost. ...I am.*

Thank you, Elly Danica, for reminding us of courage and dignity. Thank you for reminding us that the word "hope" concerns us all.

*Nicole Brossard*
*January, 1988*

*(The Introduction has been translated from the French by Louise Fleming.)*

# 1

1.1    DON'T. I only know this word. This is the only word I have ever learned. Don't. I can not write with only this word. A woman's vocabulary: Don't.

1.2    Don't tell. Don't think. Don't, what ever else you do, don't feel. If you feel, the pain will be there again. Don't.

1.3    But the pain is there anyway. It exists even when I don't. See? I warned you. You can't afford to feel. Pain will reach out of your belly and grab you by the throat. Choking. His hands around my throat. It is only pain. Old friend. I thought it was him. Again. Only pain. I can stand the pain. I can drown it in words or wine or smoke. Something can be done. If it was him again, that would be different.

1.4    Feeling. Exploring. Pain like a mountain. I climb. More pain. The mountain never ends, it grows in me daily, my belly expanding to hold it. Nothing is born of this pain. Nothing I want to hold up to the light. Monster. Monstrous. Me. Mary, Mary, quite monstrous in my belly Mary Shelley. I know what you mean. I live here too. But only just survived the ritual incisions thrice carved on my pale belly.

1.5     I know death too. Death looks like the man my mother married. His pants down. Kids don't remember. I was a four-year-old adult. I remember. I was never a kid. I don't remember being a kid. I remember nothing useful. I remember yearning for innocence. Yearning for not knowing. Four. Nine. Eleven. Twelve. Thirteen. Fourteen. Fifteen. Fifteen began the time of yearning for memory. A different memory. I don't want to remember this. This never happened. The world is dark. There is no memory. Only his hands around my throat. Blocking. Memory gone. Speech gone. Feeling gone. No I. Nothing left.


1.6     She washes dishes. She's good at washing dishes. What else do we need her for? Why should I feed her? She's useless. I'll get a dishwasher, you plug them in, they don't talk back. She doesn't talk. Talk when I tell you. Smile goddamnit. Smile or I'll fix your face so it will do what I want.


1.7     Wanting. He always wants. I don't want. Who asked you? He wants. He gets. He knows how. Hands. Beating. Choking. Screaming? Who is that screaming? That's not me screaming. I no longer know how to scream. Except inside. Co-operate or I'll kill you. Do this or I'll hurt you. I already hurt. Inside. He can't see inside. Almost victory. There is something he can't touch. Inside. Very far away. Just a little light. Inside. Almost smile. Don't. He wants. He always wants.


1.8     Don't tell. Your mother. She doesn't understand. Our secret. Every time you tell I'll hurt you worse. Remember that. This is so you'll remember to keep your mouth shut. This is so you'll do as you're told. This is because you're ugly. This is so you'll learn you are a woman. I know how to hurt you so there are no bruises. I'm not stupid. Stupid is female. Stupid cow. Stupid slut. Do what I tell you. Open your mouth. Put it in. If you bite again I'll kill you. Simple. Open your mouth. I'm already dead. What does it matter? Who will help me? My mother will not meet my eyes. My mother walks away. My mother knows. She knows. She always knows.

1.9    Children don't remember. Anyway. What does it matter? Who will believe the kid? I know what I'm doing. There are no visible bruises. Nobody will ever know. I'll kill you if you tell.

1.10    I know. Twenty-five years since the last secret. Thirty-six years since the first secret. I know. I don't know how to tell. Fear is the taste of my own blood in my mouth. Hands again. Always hands. Always hurting. Jaw. Neck. Throat. Arms. Belly. Genitals. Thighs. Always hurting.

1.11    Soul. A tiny light. If he doesn't know about it I can keep it. My secret. My soul. A self. A star. Millions of light years away. I search. I don't tell. He thinks I don't remember. He is puzzled by hate. After all he did for me. After all he gave me. I only hate. I do not murder. I have my star search. I believe in soul. He believes in hell. His own invention. He will reap what he sows.

1.12    Justice. How can I believe? He is free. I carry chains. He killed all that was beautiful in me. He is free. He has comfort. My mother. I don't know my mother. I don't know comfort. All I know is pain. Not just hands. Not just penis. Pain is like a stone growing in my belly. The mountain. I push it before me. It will never be born. Monstrous. Hate. I wear a girdle of hate. Days deformed. Life. This is not life. This is hell. The hell of the hands, choking. The hell of the penis, pushing. No. The hell of the four-year-old adult. Who doesn't remember. Who never forgets. Hate.

1.13    Hate as a promise. Never forget. Don't remember. Just never forget. Hate. Chains of hate. At least you won't forget to hate. The chains help you to remember. Bound to him. Bound to remember sooner or later. Later. I am forty. Now memory grows like a tree he planted. I hate the tree. I hate everything. When I was eleven he said he would teach me what it meant to be a woman. Again. He forgot the other times. Maybe I was a kid then. He doesn't have to remember. I can never forget.

1.14    I am not grateful. I am never grateful. Hands again. He'll teach me to be grateful. I am still not grateful. Thank it. Get down on your knees and thank it for making you a woman. That? Laughter. I'll kill you. Hands. Where is the light? Why is it so dark? Hands. My throat hurts. I can't kiss it. You can't make me. He knows how to use his hands. My throat doesn't exist. I don't exist. You can't make me. He is tired of hurting me. Go away, he says, I'll teach this lesson again. Tomorrow.

1.15    Another day. Always another day. Why doesn't he die of his evil? Only I will die of his evil. Ugliness.

Something rotten. He sees it in my face. He laughs. Look in the mirror, stupid. Boils. On my face. Why is the evil of the fathers only visited on the daughters? Why do I have boils? Why not him? He wants to carve the boils from my face. He wanted to be a doctor. They wouldn't let him. He hates 'they'. He hates me. He will fix my face. I hide. He fixed my leg once. Dug in with a pocket knife. Made a hole in the muscle. Why should he care?

1.16    Kid's got no guts. Kid's got no brains. Just a stupid cunt. I said spread them. Now! Why? Because I said so. Because that's all you're good for. Do what you're told. Aren't you ever going to learn to do what you're told? Why do you make me hurt you? Do you think I like to hurt you? Smile I said. See what I mean? You never do a goddamn thing I ask. You never do anything right. No guts. No brains. Stupid.

1.17    He says I'm stupid? What he wants is stupid. Why don't you get somebody else for your stupid games? I like you. Daddy's girl. Wanna be daddy's girl? No. Just think that. Don't say no. Say nothing. I said don't you want to be daddy's girl? I expect a yes. Say yes. Say thank you daddy. That's what he wants. Don't say it. Don't say anything. Don't be part of his evil. If you don't say yes it's only a venial sin. You have to say yes. He wants a yes. He'll get a yes. He'll use his hands to get a yes. He'll rip the hair from your head. He'll get a yes. Now it is your sin. Now it is your fault.

1.18    Memory. Process. Year of the Rabbit. Running from memory. Can't run from him. No place to run. Nobody believes he hits me. How can I make them believe the rest? Where would I go? He said he'd find me and kill me, even if I run. No hope. Only hate. Hate as a live and growing thing. Hate keeps me alive. For tomorrow: a day when somebody believes me. Dawn. Someday. All I live is night. How can you live only night? Easy. Twenty-five years of darkness. Not easy. Hate as a companion. Nobody believes me at eighteen. Twenty. Twenty-three. At twenty-five I am declared a fuck-up. Useless. Again. I vow to leave town with my hate. I vow to look for sunshine. I see a shrink. Another shrink. Another. Finally a woman. Compassion. Now hate has sewn my lips down, stitched them to my teeth. I can no longer speak. Twenty-seven. Twenty-nine. Paralysis of the will. Fuck-up. Useless. Always useless. To everybody. Even to myself. Useless.

1.19   I lose hope. Nobody believes me. Thirty. It's now or never. I learn to live with never. Never again. I don't remember. I don't want to remember. Memory pursues me. Memory uses a pen to pursue me. Memory runs out the ends of my fingers and makes marks on paper. I don't have to read this. This is useless. What does this mean? Indulgence. Sin. No right to write of how I feel. Bitter. Indulgence. Bitter, but hold on. Don't let it go. Don't let the tears come. Indulgence. A sin. The sin of the women to live only in their pain. The sin of the women never to see the universal. Stuck in the mundane. You'll never be spiritually evolved. Stuck. Making marks on paper. I never stop. I scream in frustration. I live alone. Now I can scream. And again. And again. I don't remember. Don't make me remember. You never forget. Hate has a purpose. Hate serves memory's purpose. The marks on paper weigh fifty pounds. I can't carry this weight anymore.

1.20    Nightmare. I'm awake. How can this be a dream? I wish it was a dream. I could forget if it was a dream. Please tell me this was a dream. Tell me I'm wrong. Tell me I can't remember it. Tell me it was too long ago. Tell me kids get it wrong. Tell me I don't have to remember.


1.21    Forty. The Year of the Hare. The year of light in darkness. Rebirth. Memory as talisman. The dawn of hope. Somebody believes me. I can't keep the secret anymore. The secret is killing me. Hands around my throat. Forty. Nightmares. Gray skies. March hare. Madness. I need rage. I only know how to rage at myself.


1.22    Descent again. Follow the March hare. The Goddess Inanna on a meathook in hell. Dead meat. Spread your legs, dog meat. Dead dog meat.


1.23    There is still hate. There is more. Always more. I find one shard implanted under my skin. I rejoice. I remove it with care. I try not to leave scars. I don't use a pocket knife. I try to heal the wound. Why no relief? There are two?  I will remove the second then. Still no relief. There are more? Still more?


1.24    The woman made of potshards. Pieces. Not herself. Never herself. Who is herself? Only broken pieces. Each one removed grows a new piece in its place. The wounds fester. There is no healing. The bleeding cannot be staunched. There is no healing. Fear again. The pieces cannot be removed. Can't cut out your soul. What soul?

Remember the star search? No. Only the pieces. Only the pain.


1.25    Inanna had insurance. If I'm gone too long, come for me. Who will be my insurance? Who will bribe the guardians of darkness and bring me back to the light? Who could find all the pieces? How can this be done? How can this not be done? Faith in the process. Descend. Enter. Memory.

# 2

2.1  *The First Gate.* Lunar portal. The moon. Night sky in winter. The cold within. Feeling. Can't go there. Don't go there. The feeling of frost under the fingernail. I can't see the moon. I must see the moon. I scrape the frost veil from the window. Hurry. The terror. The basement. If only I could see the moon. Everything will be alright. Nothing will be alright ever again. I need the moon. The window is clear, one small space for the moon to enter. I press my cheek to the frost. I am so cold. There is no moon. I am lost.

2.2  I yearn for someone to save me. Yearn for pity. There is no help. My grandmother is a continent, an ocean, away. I try to tell my teacher at school. She says: You are subject to your father in all things. He is your lord as jesus is your lord. He would do no harm or no wrong. He is right in all things. If you are punished or hurt it is for your own good. If he is too rough it is because he loves you. Pray to jesus for comfort.

2.3  There is no comfort so I pray for martyrdom. At least if I was dead somebody would know. If I was dead it would be over.

2.4     When I am eight he begins to use a camera again. A different sort of attention. At first I am relieved. Maybe this means he won't touch me. He yells more. Sit up. Turn your head. Wet your lips. Smile. Goddamnit I said smile.


2.5     I have a photograph of defiance from this time. Before I knew I was a victim. Before understanding began. Before I knew what he would do.


2.6     Spring. The winter is past. I have seen the moon again. I have talked to my grandmother in the moon. I have begged the virgin mary for help. I know that whatever they say in school about her son, he is deaf to the pleas of children.


2.7     I spend more time in church anyway. If I stay home the man who always wants is there, waiting for my mother to leave the house. I hate the boredom and dark droning of the church. But at least I am left alone with my thoughts. No one touches me. I think that it is all my fault. I pray to the virgin mary for strength to refuse. Strength to fight.


2.8     Spring. The winter is not past. I am nine years old. He takes three kids to the stockcar races. He meets his brother there. The field where he parks the car is muddy. The wind is raw. The day is cold. The sky a gray aftermath of storm. I look at what happens on the track from a distance. He won't let me leave his side. He has something in mind. I am not here to see the races. He sends my brother and younger sister away while he discusses with his brother how they will proceed. His brother says he already has some customers. He beckons to a farmer who has been watching us. The three of them discuss a price and what I will do. I try not to listen. I know there is no escape. I don't believe what I hear. I think this is a dream. And I wanted to go out today. This is god's punishment for not staying home to help my mother.

2.9     I am told: go with the farmer. He smells of dust and the barn. His gray striped coveralls are rough and dirty. He does not smile as he beckons me to follow. I look back at my father and his brother. My father signs that I am to go with the man. I do not know what this is about. The farmer opens the back door of a car and pushes me in. I protest. He says my father told him I wouldn't make any trouble. He doesn't have to say anymore. I am afraid. I look through the windshield and see my father watching. The farmer tells me to pull the car door closed. I am told to lie on top of him. There is no escape. I do not understand.

2.10     Memory. Body memory. My stomach hurts. I can't write this. I am afraid. I want to puke. I can smell the dust of the car seat. I can see the pattern of the upholstery. I remember running my fingernail in the grooves of the pattern while something is done to me. Now I am under someone. I think I will choke. I try not to think. I can't pray. How can this be? What is he doing? Why is he taking my panties off? Why does he want to touch me there? What on my chest could possibly interest him? Why is he on top of me? When will he be finished jiggling himself? What is he doing? Why can't he do this without me? I turn to stone.

2.11    The farmer leaves. I do not move. Mistake. There is someone else getting into the back of the car. I don't know how long it goes on. I don't know how many men there are. I don't know anything except the upholstery pattern and I know that very well. Don't see anything of the races. I spend the afternoon in the car. When I am allowed out there is only one man left waiting. He is Chinese. He is the only one daddy says no to. Daddy says it might rub off. The Chinese man might make me yellow.

2.12    I turn yellow anyway. Strange, they say. How could she have got hepatitis? There is nothing in my childhood which makes me happier. Daddy hates yellow people. Daddy will leave me alone now. I am happy for nearly six weeks. I dream of a future. Dream of a time when I can leave. I learn to love the radio. I read books and books and more books. I read fairy tales. I learn to hope that someday somebody will save me.

2.13    The spring I am nine years old I learn I am a thing. I learn girls cannot act. Somebody might save me. If I am lucky. I know I can't save myself. But it's over I think. It's over now. It's not as bad as you think. The nun told you he was right in all he did. It can't be bad. It just felt bad because you don't understand. Everybody has to do these things they don't like for daddy. But why not my sister? Why did he not let them touch my sister? Why did she not have to go into the car with the men? Don't think about that. Don't think. Stay yellow for as long as you can.

2.14   I decide that I will learn to understand. I begin to read about other children. But it is stupid. They live lives of pleasant days, children's games. I don't believe real kids live like that. Maybe those were Canadian kids, maybe when I am a real Canadian I will be able to live like that. But I am not a Canadian kid. I know that Canadian kids would never have to live with a father like mine. My father is the way he is because he comes from a stupid foreign country. I begin to look into the ways of foreign countries. I find ancient Egypt. In Egypt, they deal with thieves in this way: they crucify them upside down and beat them till they die. I am comforted. For if they do that to slaves who steal what will be the punishment for my father? What will they do to a father who does the sort of horrible things my father does? But nowhere do I read that fathers are punished for what they do to daughters. Nowhere. I lose hope. I push myself to read harder books. Nothing gives me a hint of a life like mine. Nothing is even close. There are saints, there are Alcott's Little Women and there are holy martyrs. There is nothing else. I am wrong.


2.15   I have a wicked imagination. I will be punished by god for my wicked mind. I confess evil thoughts. Bless me father for I have sinned. What evil thoughts? the priest asks. About my father I say. I don't like it when he does that. What? I don't know. That. Say ten hail mary's and five our father's and think about what you owe your father and your heavenly father. What about what they owe me? Don't be silly child. They owe you nothing. Say your penance before you leave the church. The little door closes and I hear whispers. I don't move. I wait 'til he is finished with the other penitent. Bless me father for I have sinned. Again. There is more. I think I hate my father.No absolution. You must ask his forgiveness and say another twenty hails mary's and work harder to keep your thoughts pure. Do you renounce your hatred? Yes, I say. No, I think. God will know if you don't tell the truth. Maybe the virgin mary will understand and ask forgiveness for me. Surely she will understand.

2.16    There is no one left to talk to. My aunt says the same things as the priest. He loves you. He might be rough but I know that he loves you. But what does it mean aunt, when a man touches you between your legs? It means you are a bad and dirty child and I don't want you in my house ever again. But aunt, it hurts. What does it mean? Don't you come here ever again. Filthy kid. Rotten kid. Ugly kid. Your mind is in the garbage, that's what it means. I don't want you around my kids. Don't come here again. But aunt, I don't know what it means. You heard me, now shut up with your filth.

2.17    I think that there must be more in books than I know. I get permission to go to the library downtown. There are interesting books upstairs but I am sent into the basement. Here you are dear, here are the books for children. But I don't want these. I've read most of them. You can't take out the books from upstairs until you are an adult, those books are only for adults. How old are you dear? Nine? It will be many years before you can use the adult books then dear. If there is something you really need, ask your mother to borrow it for you.

2.18    Sure. Mom? Can you get me a book that tells me why smelly fat men touch me between the legs? Mom?

Is there something that will explain this to me? Mom? Can you find me a book that explains why daddy gets money from men who make me sticky and try to kiss me on the mouth? Mom? Can you find something to tell me why they like my panties? Why I have to lift up my dress? Mom? Mom? Mommy?

2.19    Nightmare. I am being swallowed up by a hole in the dining room floor. First somebody touches me, then I am swallowed up. I land in a swamp. Everything I touch is sticky. Darkness. There is no place to put my feet. I slide in ooze. I am surrounded by black slime hanging from trees. I am sucked further and further into the swamp. I hear howling. I wake and hear myself screaming. Now I know that I am not even safe at night. My dreams contain the same monsters as my days. I begin to sleep with my prayerbook under my pillow, to ward off evil dreams. These are devil dreams because I hate. God knows I hate. God punishes, even in your dreams. I begin to feel evil, the devil's handmaiden. I am surrounded by terror.

2.20    I am glad when daddy lets me stay up late to help him. All I have to do is sit still while he takes photographs of me in my nightie.

# 3

3.1    *Second gate.* Body. Body memories. Blond child. Blue eyes. Satin skin. Beautiful child. Trust before fear. She knows he doesn't like her, but he's her daddy. When she was four she refused to let him buy her a teddy bear he promised, her mom says. But Mom, I remember what he made me do for the bear.

3.2    I don't want to remember. Why can't he just give me something? Why do I always have to do things I don't like for him? What's wrong with him? He's your father. There's nothing wrong with him.

3.3    In that other life, in Holland, he takes her to a toy store. After the first time. He offers to buy her anything in the store. But she is wise. She refuses. All the pretty things she wanted so badly a week ago she now refuses. He insists. Bears and beautiful dolls are taken from shelves and presented to her. Do you want this one? No. How about this one? No. Here's a pretty one, how about this one? No. Isn't there anything you want? No. He becomes furious. You're not leaving the store unless you choose something. No. As she leaves the store she sees a bag of marbles on the counter. This is what she chooses. She knows she can lose every single one of them and she won't have to remember what he did to her.

3.4    Heavy cotton dresses and panties. The feeling of lifting the dress over my head. The chill of the room. The feeling of being on the bedroom floor. Playing doctor with daddy. Don't tell mommy. A special game. A secret just for you and your daddy. Daddy says we can't play on the bed. Mommy would notice. Isn't it fun to have a secret from mommy?

3.5    I'm cold daddy. Here, let daddy rub you to make you warm. But daddy my back is cold, not my tummy. Don't touch my tummy daddy I don't like it. Of course you like it. If daddy kisses your little buttons they'll grow big and you'll be a big girl, all for daddy. Yes daddy. But I don't like it daddy. That's because you are a silly girl. Take your panties off. I'll warm you up some more. But daddy it's my back that's cold. If I rub between your legs your back will get warm. I don't want to daddy. Do you want daddy to get mad? No daddy. Then do what I tell you. Take your panties off so I can make you warm. But.... Do you want a spanking? No daddy. Then take them off.

3.6    I'm even colder. On my back. Daddy is exploring he says. I don't know what he wants. He tries to put his finger into me. I sit up quickly. Terrified. Hurt. I didn't know there was anything there that could hurt so much. I cry. He reaches for his handkerchief and tells me to wipe my face. He pushes me down on my back again. I clench my thighs as tightly as I can. Spread your legs. I want to see where I hurt you. Stop whimpering he says. I'm not done he says. I want to take a picture he says. I don't like this. I don't like this at all daddy. Daddy please stop. Daddy you're hurting me. You said I'd like it and I don't daddy.

23

I really, really don't like this daddy. I don't ever want to play this game again. Stop daddy. Stop hurting me. Please. Please. I'll do anything else you want but stop hurting me there. I want my mommy. Mommy!

3.7    He hits me. He hits me again. I cry louder. Mommy calls from the bottom of the stairs. She doesn't come up the stairs. I want her so much. Please mommy come up the stairs and make him stop. What's wrong she calls. Nothing. She's alright. Don't tell our secret. No daddy. Daddy will buy you anything you want. Yes daddy. Put your dress and panties on. Yes daddy. Daddy? What? It still hurts there. Don't be silly. It's all in your imagination. You don't know what you're talking about. Now go downstairs to your mother. Tell her I won't be down for awhile. I want to take a nap. Remember. It's our secret.

3.8    My world is suddenly very different. What has changed? Why do I feel so funny? Why does it hurt so much between my legs? Why did daddy want to do that? Mommy? Daddy said to tell you he's taking a nap. Mommy? Can I have a bath? Why? It's not bath day. I just finished doing all the floors. I don't want to bath you. Mommy I really need a bath. Why? Because mommy. I want a bath mommy. Please. Please can I have a bath. Please mommy. No. Go play while I make supper. Mommy? Why can't I have a bath? Maybe later. I have to make supper now. Go play for awhile.

3.9    I have never wanted so much to have a bath. I think a bath would make it feel better. I feel dirty. I want warm water to take away the memory. I want a bath so much. Mommy said a bath is still days away. I can't wait. The pail with the floor washwater stands near the doorway. I make up my mind. I back into the pail and sit in it. The water is brown and dirty, but oh, it feels good. Mommy is angry. Now she'll have to bath me after all. And what about supper?

3.10    Supper is late. Mommy says she doesn't understand why I would do such a thing. Why, when I was such a good girl, would I sit in the washwater. I start to cry. I can't stop crying. I needed a bath mommy. You wouldn't listen to me when I said I really needed a bath. But why? I promised I wouldn't tell you mommy. Daddy said you wouldn't understand. She is drying my back. She turns me to face her. What wouldn't she understand? He touched me and I didn't like it. Please don't tell him I told you mommy. Where did he touch you? Here. And here. Between my legs. He hurt me. Don't tell him I told you. I don't ever want him to touch me again.

3.11    There is fear in her eyes. He was right. She doesn't understand. She gives me some bread and jam. You are too upset to eat supper she says and takes me to my bed. It will be alright in the morning she says. Why has the world changed so much? Why am I so unhappy? Why does it feel like nothing can ever be the same again? Now daddy and mommy will be mad at me forever. It's my fault. I should not have told. I'm sure he will punish me. I cry myself to sleep.

3.12    In the morning I find a changed mommy. She tells me that I will spend a week with her parents. She and daddy have to talk. About me? Yes. About how bad I am. Yes. He says he never touched you. He calls you a liar. You've never lied to me before. I don't know who to believe. When you come back he'll have forgotten all about it. Be good at Oma's house. Don't ask so many questions. I promise to be good mommy. I promise. I didn't lie to you mommy. He did what I said he did. I'm still sore mommy. Will I always be sore there now mommy?


3.13    Grandmother's house in Amsterdam. Dark wood. Grandma's chair. Her knitting. Grandpa's pipes. The smell of furniture and floor polish. The smell of Grandma's cologne, of her dresses. A beautiful formal dining room. Red carpets on the floor and also on the table. Flowers. A home filled with old and very beautiful things. Even the light is golden here.


3.14    A very neat and tiny kitchen. I sit on a stool near her. She prepares vegetables for supper. We have just come back from a walk to the greengrocer's. She has made me a cup of cocoa and spread a thick slice of bread with butter and hagel. She tells me that I must always tell the truth. There is nothing worse than a liar. I know, Oma. I tell the truth. I never lie to mommy. I would never lie to you. But Oma, why don't people believe me when I tell the truth? This puzzles her for a few moments. Sometimes dear, people don't like the truth. Is that why daddy thinks I'm a liar? Did you lie to your mommy about daddy. No Oma.

3.15    I don't ever want to see daddy again. Can I live with you Oma? No I guess not. Opa wouldn't like it. Little kids make too much noise for him. Wouldn't you miss your mommy and your brother and sisters? Only a little bit. Mommy would visit me here wouldn't she?

3.16    I want you to tell me the truth. Pretend you are in church. You know how terrible it is to lie to jesus. Tell me the truth like you would tell jesus the truth. Yes Oma. What did daddy do? I don't want to think about it Oma. I don't want to remember. Remember. It is very important. What did he do? Do I have to tell? Yes.

3.17    I sigh. My stomach knots itself. I don't feel good Oma. Tell me. The truth. Daddy wanted to play doctor with me when mommy washed the floor. He locked the bedroom door from inside. He never did that before. He put the key in his pocket. I had to take my dress off but I got cold. He wouldn't let me put my dress back on. He wanted to rub me. I didn't want him to rub me. It was silly. I told him my back was cold and he wanted to rub my front. He wouldn't listen to me. I was so cold and he wouldn't let me have a blanket or anything. He made me take my panties off. I didn't want to. He said he would give me a spanking if I didn't do what he said. I don't like spankings. I took my panties off. He said if he rubbed me between my legs I would get warm. I didn't believe him but I was so cold. He made me lie down on the floor beside the bed. He poked between my legs with his fingers. He hurt me. I cried but he wouldn't stop. He hurt me some more there. He hit me to make me stop crying. I couldn't stop. He hit me again.

3.18   That's all Oma. Where was your mother? She was downstairs. I hoped she would come upstairs and make him stop. I cried loud so she would hear me. But she didn't come to see what was the matter. She called from the bottom of the stairs and asked if I was alright. He said yes. He wouldn't stop. Then he had a nap. And I went down and asked mom if I could have a bath. When she said no I fell accidently on purpose into the washwater pail.


3.19   I didn't tell her about the camera. I didn't believe that myself. That was too strange for anyone to believe. So now I know that I did lie to my Oma. I kept one thing from her. I wonder if it would have made any difference? She believed me. I saw that on her face. She was very upset. She told me that she would see to it that it never happened again. It would be alright to go home. He'd never do anything to me again. But since we had five more days we were going to have fun and forget all about what had happened.


3.20   Oma takes me for long walks in the park. We go to a greenhouse to look at the flowers. She loves flowers and always has them in her house. Later in the week when she sees that I am still upset, she takes me to the beach. I still don't want to go home.


3.21   She packs a thermos of tea for us and some bread and biscuits. While I play Oma sits in a large wicker beach chair from which she can watch me or work at her knitting. It is too cold to play in the water but I take my shoes and stocking off anyway and let the waves chase me.

3.22    Even the beach has changed. I feel old. Four years old. I know I don't look any older. I can not have as much fun as I once had at the beach. I no longer feel like playing. The world doesn't look the same. I don't know who to ask about this. Don't understand why. I blame whatever is between my legs. I'm not curious. I never look there. I decide now that I know how much it can hurt I will make a point of ignoring it. I decide then, for the first time, that I want to be a boy. The boys on the beach seem to have alot more fun than I do.

3.23    I tell my grandmother I want to be a boy. This upsets her. I don't like being a girl. I don't want to be a girl anymore. She asks me if this is because of what happened with daddy. Yes I say. It hurts too much to be a girl. I don't like it anymore. She stares past my head. I look in the same direction and see only sand and ocean. She does not speak to me again for a long time. So long that I am frightened. What's wrong Oma? What's wrong. She hugs me close. She still does not speak. She holds me for a long time. And then Oma promises me that what happened with daddy will never happen again. It will be alright to go home, there is nothing to be afraid of now.

3.24    At home I am the child who stands apart. The watcher. I search faces for answers to questions I dare not ask. For weeks I listen at doors, straining to hear whispered conversations. I know there are plans, but when I try to tell my sister she doesn't believe me. We are going away, far away, to a place called Canada. I know life will change, I feel it in the air, in the quality of the tension in the house. I know the changes won't be good ones, I don't understand how I know this, but I know. And I don't want to leave.

# 4

4.1    *Third Gate.* The trouble maker. The four year old trouble maker. The liar. Everything had changed in my world. I was right. My mother. What was wrong with my mother? What had he done to her while I was away? Had he hurt her too? Why did her face look all puffy like that? Why did she cry every time she looked at me? Why didn't she want me near her? Why didn't she smile anymore? What had happened while I was at Oma's in Amsterdam? Was I returned to the wrong family? What was wrong? Where was my mother? Had I remembered it wrong? Was I being punished because I didn't want to come home? Why was everything changed? What had I done that was so bad?

4.2    It was all in my mind she said. Liars can't tell the real from the not real. Kids always lie to adults. I was mixed up in my mind. She would never be able to trust me again. Once a liar, always a liar. I was to be punished for lying, but she knew it wouldn't stop me. And I was to apologize to daddy for hurting his feelings. I refused. I could not refuse. He wanted an apology. You can't make me I said. I didn't lie. I don't want to remember what he did. I didn't lie. I know where he touched me. I know what it felt like. Why should I say I'm sorry when I didn't do anything. It's not fair. I know, my mother said. But he wants an apology and it's best to give him what he wants.

4.3     I'm sorry daddy. I look at his shoes. I mumble. What? I want to hear it again. I'm sorry daddy. He grabs my chin and squeezes hard, lifting my head so I will look at him. I look at the wall behind him. I don't want to see his eyes. I know what they say. I know he is lying and that he wants me to see his victory. Get out of my sight. I can't stand liars. And don't think anybody will ever believe anything you say. You hear me? I'll make sure everybody knows what a liar you are.

4.4     Standing in front of daddy. The first time. Four years old. A liar. But I am not a liar. I try to talk to mommy. She won't have anything to do with me. Go play. My sisters won't play with me. I have upset daddy so much. And he has warned them. I look around the apartment. I wonder how I can live in this new world where nobody will talk to me. Where nobody believes me. Where my mommy doesn't love me anymore. And where daddy watches me and grins. Why is he so pleased?

4.5     My mother tells me many years later that I never played as a child. I remember becoming sullen and withdrawn. I remember staring for hours at nothing. I remember that the world no longer held any joy. It took a long time to be able to forget. I always knew when he remembered though. The grin. He was so pleased with himself. And he made a point of being cruel to me. Because of what I had done to him he said. Everything I did had to be approved by him. My behaviour had to be reported. He wanted to make sure I didn't ever lie again. If there was something I wanted he would say no. Liars didn't get anything nice. Liars didn't get treats or candy with the other kids. Liars had to pay for their lies, forever.

4.6     The myth they all believe. She is a liar. She tells terrible lies about daddy. And she is forty. She still tells the same lies about daddy. She finally tells a sister. What, her sister asks, is killing this family? Lies. Secrets. I don't believe you her sister says, you're lying. You always lie. You hate him. He's never done anything to you. You hate him because you are an evil and obnoxious bitch. A liar.


4.7     Dinner. I am thirteen. He decides he doesn't have to pretend anymore, he can do whatever he wants to me. Whatever he wants. If he says I don't eat, I don't eat. If he says I beg for my dinner on my knees beside his chair, then I beg. He walks into the room. All the children around the green table freeze in terror. He sits. He looks at me. The sullen one. The one who can no longer smile. He begins to scream at me. I ignore him. He always does this. The words are always the same. The hate in his posture, his voice, his hands. He turns to the others. Do you..., he screams at them. Do you want to grow up..., he bellows. Do you want to grow up to be like her? At the top of his lungs in a small room and me not more than three feet away. He spits. All the little faces round me wide-eyed terror and tears. No, they whimper.


4.8     He sits at the head of the table. All the best food in the house goes to him. If we touch his food he hits us. It's his food. Saturday night he has chicken and we have soup. No child at that table had so much as the grease from a chicken. It was his. He sits huddled over it, defending it from us. He sits there and chews slowly, his eyes watching the faces of the kids. He asks us if it smells good. And we say, yes daddy, it smells good. Well, he says, you can forget about it, you're not getting any.

4.9    After dinner I ask them, my little sisters, what they think I have done. They are puzzled. They don't know. It doesn't matter. Daddy said you are bad. So you are bad. Daddy said not to talk to you. Daddy said to tell him everything you say because it will be bad. Do you think I'm bad I ask them? You must be. Daddy said you are bad.


4.10    Years of being bad. Everything I did or thought. Everything I didn't do or didn't think. Everything about me was bad. It only bothered me at dinner when he screamed. It only bothered me when the little sisters I loved, hated me because he told them to. It only bothered me when they whimpered. No daddy, I don't want to be like her. No daddy I won't ever tell lies like she does. I'll always do what you tell me to do daddy.


4.11    Forty. Still bad. Still hating. Still telling lies. And siblings in their thirties still believe him. They trust him. They don't trust themselves and they still hate me for the pain I have caused him. I have tried to tell several of them what he did. I don't get disbelief. I get shocked outrage. How could I do this to him? How could I even think this about him? How could I be such a mean and awful bitch? Daddy would never do anything like that, he couldn't even hurt a fly. Such a wonderful daddy. Such a sensitive daddy. Such a good daddy. We love our daddy so much. And we still hate you. He was right. He was always right about you.


4.12    Forty. No comfort. A trouble maker. Always. A liar. Always. A brother says I can say whatever I want, that is my right as an adult. He knows that I speak only lies. He learned long ago not to trust me. Who taught you I ask. No one, he says, I just know about you. Nothing you say will make any difference to me he says. A trouble maker.


4.13    A sister: how could you? How could you even think that about him? My daddy. No wonder he hates you. How did you ever get to be so evil? I don't want you near my kids. My husband knew you were a trouble maker the first time he met you. We don't want your kind around here. What kind? Troublemaker. Man hater. Liar.


4.14    To another sister: don't you think I might have a reason to hate men? Don't you think somebody taught me to hate? No, she says. You were born bad. He was right. What did any man ever do to you? They can't stand you. It's no wonder. Liar. Trouble maker. Man hater.


4.15    Another sister: learn to be a lady. Keep your mouth shut. He hates you because you provoke him. You don't know how to handle him. I do. He doesn't hate me. Only you, because you never learned to keep your mouth shut. I never learned to do what I was told either, I say. Right, she says. What do you expect him to do? You give him no choice but to hate you. He hates you because you aren't grateful. Grateful? For what he did for you, stupid. You deserve hatred. At least you could pretend to be grateful. Then he wouldn't have to hate you.

4.16  My mother: you don't understand him. I used to be afraid of him. I'm not afraid of him anymore. You know he vacuums for me sometimes. He helps me with the dishes now. I don't want to be alone. He's all I have. What about your children I say. What about them, she says. He hurt you, I say. Kids always exaggerate, she says. I know he hurt you. I saw him hurt you. He's always been a good husband. I'm not as afraid of him as I used to be. When did you stop being afraid of him? She looks away. Oh, she says, a couple of years ago I guess.

4.17  I give my mother a book. She handles it as though it is radioactive. What is it, she asks. It is letters between mothers and daughters. I thought you might like it. You wrote to your mother for thirty-five years. I thought you might like to read what other women wrote to each other. She already knows it is a trap. Dangerous. But she is touched. You can't afford this she says. I can't afford not to I say. She looks at the dedication. I see tears on her face. I can't take this she says. Why? Because of what it says. He wouldn't understand. Who? Your father. No, your husband. I want to honour my mother with a gift. It has nothing to do with him. You have to change this she says. I can't take it like this. He wouldn't understand. You don't know him.

4.18  The dedication says: To my mother. I always loved you, always. I used her maiden name and signed it with my chosen name. Wanting to keep him out of it. Wanting something just between us, without him. I don't know how to describe the terror on her face. She is sixty-two years old. She has lived all her adult life in fear of the

35

man she married. She is still afraid. The book is a bomb. In it daughters tell their mothers about fathers raping, fathers beating. I hope she will read at least one hundred pages. I know she will not even open it. I don't know if she took it home. She never speaks about it again.

# 5

5.1    *Fourth Gate.* Daddy wants you. Why? He wants you to say goodnight to him. Why? He's in the basement. Say goodnight to your father. The basement. I am ten. Each night I must go into the basement before I go to bed. In my nightdress, barefoot, I stand outside the darkroom door. Goodnight daddy. If I am lucky the door is closed and stays closed.

5.2    Sometime that year he begins to build what he calls a studio. He does not say what it is for. His father helps him. We are not allowed to go near it without permission. I have permission to help my mother clean it. I find strange clothes in the dressing room. What's this Mom? Nothing. Mom, this stuff is weird. What's it for Mom? Nothing. Don't touch it, it's dirty. Black and red lacy things. Lipstick that does not belong to my mother. A crusty pair of panties. I ask her again. With great bitterness she replies. Those are his props.

5.3    Whatever goes on in the basement I don't know about it. I am curious. One night a party downstairs wakes me. There are sounds of laughter. Men and women. Sounds of drinks being made. I hear my mother in the kitchen so I quietly go to the top of the stairs and position myself so that I can see her walk between the kitchen and the living room. She carries plates of snack foods. Returning with empty glasses she thinks she hears something and comes to the bottom of the stairs to check. I have anticipated her and move out of sight. When she goes back to the guests I return to my lookout ledge.

5.4     The party moves into the basement. I see a troop of men and one woman other than my mother. My mother does not go with them into the basement but stays behind to clean up. I watch her walk back and forth for a time before I decide there is nothing else to see. I go back to bed.

5.5     This becomes routine. There are different women, but usually the same few men. Sometimes my mother goes into the basement with them. They always begin the party in the living room. When they have had several drinks they go into the basement studio. After a time they return to the living room for coffee and then they leave. In the morning, floating in plastic photographer's trays, there are proof sheets from the night before. Large-busted naked women. Women I have only seen from my perch at the top of the stairs. Women I never see again.

5.6     It is my job, in the morning, to make up my parents' bed. I find a book under his pillow. Pictures of naked women. Pictures with the same sort of lacy things I had seen in the basement. I don't know what this means. I ask my mother. The book belongs to your father. Don't touch it. But, I reasoned, I could look at it. I could hardly make up the bed without touching the book he left under

his pillow. He'd never know as long as I didn't say anything to my mother. Now there is always a book under
his pillow. A different book every few days. I look at them
all, trying to make sense of this. It takes longer and longer
to make up the bed.


5.7     I did not connect the photographs in the sink with
the ones in the books. Until today. I know what he is now.
A pornographer. Scum of the earth. Pimp and pornographer. He used my mother. He used the wives of some
of his 'friends'. He used young women he enticed with
stories of fame and fortune. He liked waitresses. He had
them all sign releases, or since one or two of them were
too young, he had their parents sign a release. He loved
women he said. He loved them all. He used them all. He
sold them all.


5.8     He begins his training of me. Sunday afternoon.
My mother instructs me before I go to the basement. He
wants you to wear the blue sweater and your corduroy
skirt. Do what he says. Don't ask any questions. Why?
Just do what he says. I am eleven.


5.9     My body is changing. I will soon be twelve. He is
very interested. Lift your shirt. What? Lift your shirt. I want
to see if you are normal. Normal? He pinches the area around
my nipples. He seems disappointed. Get of my sight.


5.10    I go to the bathroom and lock the door. I try to
look at myself in the mirror. The mirror is too high and

I have to stand on the toilet across the room from it. I can see nothing at all. I can't see anything by looking down at myself. Except that there seems to be something growing on my chest. Something he thinks isn't normal. I am afraid. Will I turn into some kind of monster? It does not occur to me that I am growing into my woman's body. It does occur to me that I hate what is happening to me if it means daddy can demand that I lift my shirt for him.

5.11　The basement. Now I find him waiting for me in the studio. I hear him moving lights, but I pretend I don't. I stand before the door of the darkroom and say good night very softly and then I scurry past the studio door and back up the stairs. I am more and more afraid of the basement.

5.12　I become bolder. For several nights I do not go to the basement before I go to bed. He notices. He threatens me. You goddamn well will come and say goodnight to me, when I say, where I say. I am frightened. Yes daddy. But I didn't want to bother you daddy. I'll say good night to you before you go into the basement. It's about time I start to teach you to do what you're told. Your mother's too soft on you. Do you understand me? Tonight, when you are ready for bed, you will say good night to me in the basement.

5.13　He is ready for me. He is in the darkroom, but to-night the door is open. Come here, he says. I want to show you something. He takes a key from his pocket and opens a small cabinet which hangs on the wall beside the door.

He removes a yellow Kodak paper box and selects some photographs. He spreads them out on the counter. My mother. Naked. Smiling that smile I know. The smile I have learned to make for the camera too. The smile I make when he says, wet your lips, lift your head, smile. The clenched teeth. The eyes of the hunted facing the camera. Caught. Powerless. Smile.

5.14    I am ashamed. Afraid. Oh no I say. This can't be right. My mother would never do this. Don't be stupid he says. She does whatever I tell her to do. Just as you'll learn to do what I tell you. Does mom like you to take pictures of her naked? She doesn't have to like it. She does what's she's told. And she knows what will happen if she doesn't. I'll send these to her old man. The old man will probably fall over with a heart attack. Serve him right. She knows. She does what she's told. I watch him replace the photos in the box in the cabinet. He locks it and the key goes back into his pocket. Wait for me in the studio he says.

5.15    He comes into the studio and switches on a few of the lamps. He fiddles with the camera. He seems to be thinking. I stand near the door. I watch him. It's past my bedtime daddy. I'll kiss you good night now. He looks at me with contempt. You'll go when I say you can. He fiddles with the camera some more, checks the settings, cocks the shutter. He moves a bench onto the backdrop paper. Come here.

5.16    I pretend I don't know what he means. Come here when I tell you, goddamn it. Where daddy? Lean over the bench? I am stupid. I don't know what he means. I won't let myself know what he means. He grabs me by the shoulder. Hands like a vise. He pushes me over the bench so that my belly can feel the plastic cover through my nightdress. I hear the camera click. Drop your panties. Don't get up. Reach behind you and pull them down. Click. My panties are around my knees. Click. Lift up your nightie. It is a struggle to stay bent over the bench. Don't turn around. Why does he sound breathless? I lay like this, with my bare ass in the air, for it seemed like forever. Daddy I want to go to bed. Shut up. Don't move. I look at the floor. The footprints on the gray background paper. Whose footprints? This is boring and stupid. What is he doing behind me?

5.17    I am not ready when it begins. The first hit sends shock waves through my whole body. My stomach contents lurch toward my throat. This is so you'll learn to do what you're told. This is so you won't ask stupid questions. This is so you'll learn to co-operate. It is the first time. He hits hard. He uses his hands. It doesn't last long. Get up. As I get up he slaps my face once hard. Take your panties and get out of my sight. Move it. Now. I whimper. I am too stunned to cry. I don't understand. I did everything he told me to do, even when it was stupid. I stop at the door. He is rewinding the film, he takes the film from the camera and slips it into his pocket. Daddy? Why did you hit me? Because you deserve it. Because I like it. I can do whatever I like. You understand me? Get up to bed. Don't bother your mother. Go straight to bed. I hold onto my tears until I reach my bed and I cry myself to sleep.

5.18　The next morning he is very pleased with himself. He asks to see me in his bedroom. I don't want to look at him. I don't want to talk to him. What does he want now? I'm ready now. He'll never catch me unawares like that again. Have you learned your lesson? What lesson? I don't know why you hit me. I didn't do anything wrong. I did exactly what you said to do. I did all the stupid things you wanted. Why did you hit me? Because you're stubborn and stupid. Because you don't do what you're told. Yes I do. Yes I do. His face is a mask with a sneer. Tonight he says. Tonight we'll see if you do what you're told.


5.19　Forty. I sit here shivering. I want to throw up. What is wrong with me? Why am I so nauseated? What brings so much fear? I write about the past. Almost thirty years ago. Why do I feel so sick writing this? Why am I so cold?

# 6

6.1     Fifth Gate. No. No. No! Don't make me think about it again. Don't make me have to feel it. Don't. Oh please don't. I can't bear it. Everything hurts. My stomach. My head. Tension in knots tightening.

6.2     Music. Mozart. Fill the space around the pain with music. Protection from the echoing haunt of pain.

6.3     Eleven. Music. Music to relax you he said. He had wired up a speaker in the studio. Music to rape by. Music to rape a child by. Relax he said. Listen to the music. Pretend you are somewhere else.

6.4     No amount of pretending could take me out of the glare of the photo lamps. No pretending could erase him. Practise he said. Pretend you are on the beach. I hate the beach I said. Do what you're told. You always liked the beach. Not anymore. Never again. He taught me to hate everything. You liked to go to the beach with the old lady. Pretend you're at the beach. No.

6.5     No and no and no! Doesn't anybody care? I don't

like this. Don't touch me. Don't touch me. Bend over the bench he says. Again? Why now? You'll learn to co-operate. You'll learn to do as you're told. I hate you. I hate you. Hands. Again. Hands. I am so hurt. On your back he says. The concrete floor. Or I'll hit you again. No! Is that me screaming? He turns up the music. Hands hitting, hitting, hitting. Now, lie on your back. Over there, on the floor. Shut up and do what I tell you. No! No! You can't make me. Oh yes, I can make you. Don't kid yourself. I can make you do whatever I want he says. I'll tell somebody! I can't take this anymore.

6.6    Who will you tell? Do you think anybody will believe you? Do you know what they do to kids who tell lies? I'll see you locked up. I'll make sure they throw away the key. I'll see you never get out. You're not going to put me in jail, I don't believe you. Not jail stupid. A place for crazy women. A place where they'll keep you forever if I tell them you're crazy. I'm your father, they'll believe me. They'll never believe you.

6.7    The nuns took me and several other kids to the asylum to hear Mass with the inmates. He wanted me to go. He said it would be good for me. I didn't know what he meant then. I was separated from the group somehow. An orderly sent to take inmates back to the ward insisted I move along. I knew the doors would lock behind me. I cried for the nuns, for rescue.

6.8    Don't let those stupid nuns tell you anything. I'm your father I can do whatever I want to you. If I say you are to be locked up, you will be locked up. If I say you're crazy, you're crazy. Now, do I have to hit you again or are you going to do what I tell you? Do you understand me? Do you? He talks to me and twists my arm until I think it will snap out of the socket. I am so sore. I am so tired. I know I can't win. I don't want to be locked up. I don't think I am crazy. I don't know how I can run. Don't know who I can get to believe me.


6.9     Daddy's always right. I must be wrong. This must be the way the world is for girls. I wish I could stop fighting. Maybe it wouldn't hurt so much if I stopped fighting. Maybe if I tried to do what he wanted he would be nice to me. Maybe if I do what he wants he'll stop hitting me.


6.10     Pretend he says. Pretend you are a woman. Pretend you really want me. Want you? You want me to do this to you don't you? Oh yes daddy. I'm good to you aren't I? Yes daddy. You love it when your daddy makes love to you don't you? You love what daddy's teaching you? Daddy has so much loving to give to a woman. Pretend you are daddy's woman. A hand squeezes my shoulder at the base of my throat. Before he makes the world go dark again he says: say you like it. I turn my head away from him. He is on top of me. There is no place to go. The hand at my throat releases the pressure for a moment. He turns my head toward him, forces me to look at him. Say it! My teeth are clenched. I hurt everywhere. I am so tired. I don't think I can fight anymore. I am not crazy. The hate in his hard eyes. The way his mouth spits venom at me. Say it bitch, or I won't be responsible for how hard I'll hit you. Say it! I can't move my head. His hand squeezes my jaw, hard. The pain shoots into my shoulder blades. Say it. Oh yes daddy, I like it a whole lot. I sneer at him. I say it. I don't give him what he wants. He slaps my face hard, harder. Again. Again. Again. I no longer know how to cry. It isn't any use to cry.

6.11   We have a ritual now. I must wait for him in the studio, leaning over the bench. He wants to warm me up he says. He is teaching me he says. This is what it means to be a woman. Drop your panties. Lean over the bench. Take your beating. Don't whimper and snivel. Don't cry. If you cry he beats harder and longer. It pleases him to hit you. He looks forward to it. Don't turn around. He doesn't want you to see how much it pleases him.

6.12   After the beating. Lie down. On your back. Take your nightie off first. Why do I have to tell you every time? You should know by now. I make him tell me. Drop your panties. Take off your nightie. I am too stupid to know what he wants. I don't remember what he said yesterday. He has to keep hitting me. Someday I'll remember what he told me. Someday I will remember.

6.13   Each time is a battle. I resist as much as I dare. I don't want to earn a harder beating. He will beat me whatever I do. If he doesn't like what I do he will be even more vicious. All I can do is try to keep him from killing me. Eleven. I know every move he makes and what it will mean for me. I know everything he likes and how not to give in to him. I make him force me. I will not give him anything he doesn't force or hit out of me first. I make it as difficult as I can. He pontificates about the stupidity of all women. But never has he known anyone as stupid as I am. He beats me for stupidity. He beats me for resistance. He beats me for stubbornness. He beats me because I don't co-operate. He beats me for insubordination. He beats me because I withhold as much as I can from him. He beats me because he likes hitting me.

6.14    I fight him with everything I have and know. When he tells me I am crazy I no longer have anything left to fight with. I become sweet. I become willing. I try to please. That's better he says. It took you long enough to learn. I vow to do anything he wants from now on. I will not be locked up. Oh no. I want to live. I don't want to be locked away from life and my dreams.

6.15    I learn to pretend. I pretend I am dead. Only my head is alive. Only a small part of my head. I have no body. There is nothing alive below my chin. I find it strange that even when I pretend it is dead and doesn't matter to me anymore my body still won't co-operate with him. I can't make my thighs unclench. He pries my legs apart every time. I wince every time he touches me. He beats me for that. I try harder not to wince. I try harder not to move away from him. I try harder not to feel. It doesn't matter what I feel anyway. And when I feel it hurts. I don't want the beatings to hurt. I learn not to feel. I succeed. I can pretend I am dead.

6.16    Upstairs I am a child with no memory. There is no day to walk through. I am a zombie. I try to hide my body from myself. My mother says I have become unco-operative. She complains about my sullen days. Nobody asks me about my nights. I am silent. I have lost the ability to speak. He said if I told anybody he would have me locked up for being crazy. Or he would kill me. I no longer have the courage to speak about anything. Darkness. She is so bad she won't do anything that daddy says. Darkness. Daddy's face. Daddy's hands. Daddy's mouth. Daddy's penis. Goodnight daddy. Goodnight.

# 7

7.1    *Descent. Fifth Gate.* I remember it was a Saturday. Afternoon in the basement. Getting ready. I don't want to remember. He is too sweet and nice to me. What does he want now? Something special tonight? What? I want you to do me a favour tonight he says. Oh, that. Now it's a favour? Now I have a choice?


7.2    Important friends. Tonight. I want you to pose for them. Just pose. Just pose? Just? I want you to do exactly as you are told. I don't want any argument or back talk. Just do what I tell you, when I tell you. These men are very important. A judge, a lawyer, a doctor. I won't leave you alone with them. You don't have to worry about that. Some fathers do that and their girls get all messed up. Me, I'm responsible. I stay in the room with the kid. That way I don't have to deal with bullshit from the kid's mother.


7.3    What does he mean? Messed up? Messed up how? What's going to be messed up? Do you understand me? he asks. I think you know what happens when you don't do what you're told, I think you know that by now. Maybe I should give you a spanking so you know what I mean eh? No, better not have any marks on you, they wouldn't like that. Go back upstairs and help your mother. She'll call you when I'm ready. Tonight.

7.4     This is the one I most want to forget. This is the time it all came apart. This was the night of my death. Eleven. Beautiful girlchild. A bright and charming elf. She wants to be an archaeologist. She dreams of a life of her own. She wants to be a writer.

7.5     Saturday supper. Bread and soup for the kids. Roast chicken for daddy. Watch him eat. Don't get caught watching. You know you can't have any chicken. Don't even dream about it. Clean up. Be quick. Company for daddy tonight. Be quiet. Do the stove and the counters again. Company tonight, everything must be spotless. He wants to check the work. Don't let him find anything undone or done badly. Be quick. He is impatient.

7.6     Bath time. First the little ones. Be quick. Be quiet. Get those kids to bed goddamn it. Hurry up I said. The older kids bath themselves. I bath last. No fresh bath water tonight. A clean nightdress. No you can't stay up. Go to bed. I'll come for you when he wants you. But Mom, I won't be able to sleep. Try, she says.

7.7     I do sleep. She wakes me. Come, she says. He wants you now. Barefoot. Cold. Walking behind my mother. Into the basement. Laughter. Are they having a party? Be quiet. Do what he says. Don't talk unless he tells you to. Do exactly what he says.

7.8　My mother opens the door of the studio. Three men. Strangers. And my father. They watch every move I make. Why are they so interested? I notice they all have drinks. They laugh when I rub the sleep from my eyes. I am dazed. I don't understand why I am here. I stand near the door. My mother sits on a chair in the corner, behind the camera. He is preparing the camera and joking with the men. He switches on the photo lamps. Sit on the bench he says. Face the camera. The men behind the camera snicker. One man chews a cigar. They lift their drinks. I try to make eye contact with my mother. Laughter. Move your head and shoulders so you face the door. Now turn your head back. Wet your lips. Again. Smile. Click. Tilt your head. Click. Open your mouth alittle. Click. Wet your lips again. Hold it right there. Click. Smile. Smile I said. Click. The glasses are refilled. I am awake now. Click.


7.9　Take your nightie off. I think he is joking. I look at him puzzled. In front of company? Take the damn thing off before I do it for you. Click. Laughter. Fear. What is this? I look at my mother. She has turned to stone. Her eyes are not focused. She will not look at me. Well, are you taking it off? I don't have all night. Slowly I lift the nightdress over my head. Click, click, click. Put your hands under your breasts. Breasts? I don't have breasts. On your chest stupid, hold your hands under your nipples then. Lift your head. Look at me. Click. Click. The men sigh. The men laugh. Cute. Turn your shoulders again. Put your left hand behind your head. Stick out your chest. Ah. Ahhh. Cute. Click. Click. Now both hands behind your head. Chest out. Turn the shoulders a bit. Turn your head away. Tilt your head up. Smile. Click. Click. Click. Lean your right elbow on the arm of the bench. Bring your knees up on the bench. I can't figure this one out. He moves from behind the camera. He sets me up. Moves me like a doll. Hold that. Wet your lips. Don't move. Click. Click. Tilt your head. Smile. Smile. Click. Relax.

7.10   He reloads the camera. The men joke and laugh. The men are pleased. The man with the cigar rubs his hands together. He is excited. The other men tease him. He is having a wonderful time. The drinks are refilled. The camera is ready. The men are ready. I am not ready.

7.11   Take your panties off. Slowly. Like I showed you. No. Do I make myself clear? Take your panties off. No. No. Mom? No answer. Mom? She looks at me finally. Do what he says. I do nothing. My mother has a whispered conference with him. I hear her say she will make coffee for later. He gives his permission. She leaves. Now take them off. Stupid kid. She can't do it with her mother watching. They're so stupid about their mothers. You know what will happen if you don't do what you're told? You remember what we talked about this afternoon? You remember your promise? Promise. I never promised you anything. Don't say that. If you say what you're thinking he'll hurt you. Slowly, so slowly, the panties come off. He doesn't notice that my skin comes off with them. I peel myself out of my own skin. I am no longer myself. I am someone else. Someone I don't want to be. Someone I don't want ever to remember having been. Someone I used to know sits on a white brocaded bench, under photo lamps, in front of a camera. A body sits here naked. The body tries to cover itself. Its hands move automatically. It clenches its thighs. It stares at the heat duct on the ceiling. It focuses on the little t-bar which controls the opening and closing of it. It hears the furnace. Now it can watch the dust blown out of the duct. It hears nothing else.

7.12    In the distance the sound of the camera. Click. Click. Click. The men seem to be silent now. The body doesn't hear the new orders given it. They are repeated several times. The body moves automatically. Spread your legs. The legs spread. Put your hand between your legs. The body puts its hand on the leg. The legs clench together. Laughter. Not like that stupid. Spread your legs again and put your hand between them. The body is too stupid to do this right. He comes from behind the camera. He snarls at the body. Snap out of it he says, or you'll be sorry. Real sorry. Do I make myself clear? You hear me? Do you hear me?

7.13    The body is no longer capable of response. The voice was peeled away with the skin. Give her a good stiff drink. She needs a drink. The body sees a drink being poured by one of the men. He gives it the drink. It sniffs the drink and makes a face. Take it all in one gulp somebody says. It drinks and chokes. Coughing brings tears. Here, wipe your face on this. Let's give her a couple of minutes. The drink should loosen her up. How much did you give her anyway? Three fingers of CC. That ought to do it. Laughter. They refill their own drinks. The body, naked and shivering, sits on the bench. The body searches for escape. One of the men sits in front of the door. He tilts his chair and rocks on it. No escape. The alcohol begins to work. Nausea.

7.14    Daddy I don't feel good. Never mind about that, it's the whiskey he says. You'll start to fell good pretty quick. Then we'll have  alittle  fun. He turns to the men. Are you ready for alittle fun, your honour? You bet I'm ready. Say when, says the man in the brown suit. He removes his jacket. He wears a vest with a large gold watchchain. The body wonders if he would let it look at the watch. The chain is pretty. The body looks at the chain. It can't make itself look at the man. He has been smoking a fat cigar. Now he chews it, moving it from side to side in his mouth. He rubs his hands together. Say when.


7.15    I'll just have a word with her and get her ready. Then it's all yours. He's going to kiss you he says. You don't have to be afraid. I'll stay right here. He won't hurt you. I'll be right here watching. Be nice to him, he just wants to kiss you alittle bit. Because he likes you. And remember what I told you. You know what will happen to you if you don't co-operate.


7.16    The man walks around the lamps towards the body, stepping over the cables. He is excited, his eyes shine. Half way across the room he laughs and turns back. Here, he says to the young man in the blue suit, hold my cigar. I don't want anything in the way of this. When he laughs the watchchain jiggles on his belly. He pulls the sides of his vest down. He is ready.


7.17    The body tries to focus on him. He is ugly. It doesn't want to look at his face. It looks at the watchchain. It looks at his shoes. He puts his finger under the body's chin and lifts its head. You're a nice girl he says. Give me a little kiss. The body turns its head away. He kisses its shoulder. He is unsteady and sits beside the body on the bench. He touches it. The body tries to move away. He moves closer. Here, give us a little kiss, that's a good girl. The body clenches its teeth and holds itself away from him. He tries again. The body gags. He is taken aback. Let me look at those pretty titties then. A hand like a claw touches the body's chest. Yellow fingernails scratch around the body's nipples. Doesn't that feel good? The body tries to cover itself. His other claw holds the wrists like a shackle. He pokes around the body's chest some more. Tries to poke his claw between its legs. He hurts it with his long fingernails. He pushes the body back against the armrest. The body's back feels like it will break. He is heavy. His breath smells of cigar and whiskey. He gets up and pulls the legs out from under it so that the body is flat on its back on the bench. The head is wedged against the arm-rest. He stands to take off his vest and waddles across the room to place it on the chair. The body does not move. It watches as he unbuttons his fly and takes something out of his pants. A tiny limp sausage. He gives it a shake. What's he going to do with it? Is he trying to wake it up?

7.18    He wobbles across the room toward the body again. He seems to be trying to throw the pink sausage he holds in his hand against the body's thighs. The look on his face says he is not pleased. Whatever it is he expects to happen is not happening. The father and the man in the blue suit suggest the body should be moved to the floor. It is very cold. It complains of the cold. Somebody gives it the nightie and the body tries to pull the nightie on. They laugh. We're not done yet. Put the nightie on the floor. Lie down on the nightie.

7.19    The body lies down on its belly. The men are talking. They'll help him and then they'll have their turns. Somebody moves the bench out of the way. The father slaps the body. Roll over on your back. He crouches near the head. If you do what you're told, this won't take long. Close your eyes and do whatever I tell you. I'm right here. Nobody will hurt you. You don't have anything to be afraid of. I don't want any of your stupid whining. I'm going to hold you right here and you're going to behave exactly as I've taught you. Do you understand me?


7.20    He holds the body down. Hand on its right shoulder. Thumb pressing at the base of its throat. Its hands held above the head. The body stretched out. She won't give you any trouble this time your honour. Hand like a vise at the throat. Bring your knees up. Trapped wrists. Can't move. The body tries to move the torso out of the way. He spreads its legs. The man is between the body's legs. He tries to put something into it. It feels his finger nails and it screams. He's hurting me, he's hurting me. The body moves its head from side to side, crying, screaming. No. No. No! Shut up a voice snarls. No. No. No! He slaps its face, hard. The head feels like it will roll away from the body with the force. He slaps it again. Now shut up. If you make a fuss it will take longer. Shut up. No. No. No. It tries to get away. It can't move. The hand at the throat. It chokes. They don't stop. The man in the blue suit crouches near the father. He holds the body's wrists. Puts his other hand over its mouth. The man between its legs is breathing funny. Suddenly he stops, he collapses on top of the body. It is over. At last it is over.

7.21   The body's hands are released and the hand over the mouth is removed. The father still holds the body by the shoulders. The men talk over the body. It looks at the faces above it. They are negotiating something. The man in the blue suit will now have his turn. The body thinks he has a nice face. It hopes he won't hurt it. He removes his jacket and hangs it on the back of a chair. He kneels at the body's feet. He leans over and kisses it on the mouth. Kisses the chest. The body's legs are clenched. Pull your knees up he says, that's a good girl. I want to have a look he says. He spreads its legs apart. Again. It's going to happen again. He's going to do the same thing as the other man. What is this? Why do they want to hurt me? Why can't they leave me alone?


7.22   It hurts. I cry. It hurts. It hurts. It hurts so much. Please daddy don't let them hurt me anymore. Shut up. He's not hurting you. Shut up and lie still. Hand over the body's mouth again. This man hurts more than the other one did. He pushes into the body. Harder and harder he pushes into it. It feels like something is ripping. The body thinks it will die. It hurts so much. The hand over its mouth barely muffles its screams. It chokes. It bites. It bites as hard as it can. He takes his hand away. The body throws up. He hits again. Somebody gives him a magazine to throw over the puke.


7.23   It's over. He gets up. The father lets go of the body, my body. I don't move. I can't move. I want to die. I hear them talking. They are trying to talk the other man into taking his turn. He doesn't seem to want to. They discuss who will hold me down. They come back to me. It's not over.

The other man and my father will have a turn. So it's fair I hear them say. Fair.


7.24    I am dead. The third man does what the other two did. He is not as rough, but I am so sore it doesn't matter. Everything hurts. Everything. Please let it be over soon. Please daddy. Please god. Please somebody, let this be over soon. Shut up. Shut up I said. The man with the watchchain and the man with the blue suit crouch at my head. They hold me down for the third man. Then they hold me down for my father.


7.25    There is murder in my father's eyes when I see him on top of me. Bitch. Stupid whining bitch. I'll show you who's in charge here. I'll show you. And he pounds into me. You give it to them and you'll give it to daddy too. I guess I should not have bit him so hard. Bitch. He hits me. I taste blood, my own blood. He hits me again. The men who are holding me protest. Hey, they say, take it easy. He takes longer than the others. I am so sore. I try to pull away from him, try to close my thighs so he can't get at me. It's no use. No use at all.


7.26    They let me go and they button themselves back into their suits. They congratulate each other. Fantastic. Fantastic. The prints will be ready for them Monday. They pay no attention to me. I am huddled into a ball on the concrete floor. I have my hands between my legs holding on. I am so sore, so sore. I want to die. I cry as loud as I dare. I don't want him to hit me anymore. Not all of the men have left. My father is discussing negatives with the man he calls your honour. The man wants to make sure he gets them all. You understand he says, a man in my position. Oh I understand perfectly says my father. I roll over so I can look at them. I see my father turn to look at me with disgust.

7.27    He says, how would your honour like to have her whenever you want? The man says he can't afford many nights like this one. He says, she's a good worker. I trained her myself. She could help your wife around the house. What do you mean? He says he would consider selling me. But what would your wife say? he asks my father. Nothing. She has lots of girls, she wouldn't miss one.

7.28    I look at the man carefully. I look at my father. I don't believe I hear him say this. The words are etched in my brain. I remember the look on his face, the sneer when he looked at me huddled on the floor crying. I remember the man's response. My wife wouldn't understand he said, she's not like your wife. You have to slap them good now and then, so they know who's boss my father says. Oh, the man said. He looks at me again. How much then?

7.29    Four hundred dollars. The man gasps. That's an awful lot of money. I don't have that kind of cash around. My father shrugs. I look at the man and think I would rather go with him than stay with a man who says he is my father, who hits me, and who is prepared to part me from my mother and sisters for four hundred dollars. Life couldn't get any worse. I'd learn to like what the man wanted from me. I'd learn to please him and his wife.

I didn't think he'd hit me. The man continues to stare at me. He'd like to he said but he couldn't come up with that kind of money. His wife was sure to notice it.


7.30    Two hundred dollars then. No, he says, his wife wouldn't understand. He seems saddened by this fact. Well then, my father says, I'll give her to you. I wouldn't do this for anybody except you your honour. You don't have to tell anybody. It will be a deal just between you and me. She can go into your house as a helper for your wife. Nobody will know. I want somebody to take her off my hands. It doesn't matter what you do with her. She doesn't complain. If she tries to complain hit her hard and she won't give you any more trouble. I've trained her myself. She does what she's told. She's a good worker.


7.31    She's a nice little piece alright. I'd really like to. I don't think I can get my wife to take her in though. You don't know my wife. It wouldn't work. I'd like to, but I know it would never work. I'm sorry.


7.32    My father shrugs. The man lets himself out of the studio. My father goes to the camera and removes the film. He looks over at me. Get up. Go to bed. I'll deal with you tomorrow.

# 8

8.1    *Fifth Gate of Hell. The Studio.* He leaves. I don't move until I hear the darkroom door close behind him. I try to get up. My legs won't support me. I roll over and lift myself onto my knees. I can't move any further than this. I am so tired. So sore. So cold. He turned the lights out as he left. The only light remaining is from the dressing room. I look at it for a long time. I try again to get up. I fall. It is too cold to stay on the floor. I have to get up. I crawl toward the light. I haul myself up, use the door to support me. Nausea. I think I will fall again. Too dangerous. Hang on. Use the wall for support. Slowly. Move slowly so you don't fall again. Don't let him find you here. Bed. How far is it to my bed?

8.2    I find the stairs. I crawl on my hands and knees, nightie in one hand. It stinks. I don't want to wear it. I make it to the bathroom. I lock the door. And then I throw up. I try to close my eyes. I throw up again. I am on the floor beside the toilet. The house is quiet. I want a bath. I don't dare take a bath. I feel too sick to move. I still have the nightdress in my hand. I use it to wipe my face but the smell of it makes me throw up again. I push it as far away as I can. I lie between the toilet and the outside wall of the house. I am so cold. I have to move before he comes upstairs and finds me. I don't want to see him ever again. I don't want him to find me here.

8.3     I want to wash myself. I want to get their smell off my body. I want to wash between my legs. Hurry. Hurry. He might come up the stairs any minute. The door is locked. He'll make me open it for him. Hurry. The washcloths are over the bathtub. I don't know if I can get up. I don't know if I can reach them. I have to. I have to. Hurry.


8.4     Hot water. Oh I will stay here forever and put warm washcloths where it hurts. My face looks terrible in the mirror. Who is it who looks back at me? I don't know who that girl in the mirror is. Where is me? Why don't I see myself in the mirror? I hear him climb the basement stairs. Too late. He bangs on the door. What are you doing in there? Nothing. Didn't I tell you to get to bed. Get out of there and get to bed. Now! You hear me? Now!


8.5     Bed. I can't sleep. I don't want to sleep. I want to think about what this means. I don't want to think at all. There is no moon to help me tonight. The street below my window is deserted. The men are gone. There is no sound from my parents' bedroom. One or two of my sisters snore. Somebody turns over and bedsprings complain. I pull the blanket around me. I can't stop shivering. I can't get warm. The room is dark. My world is dark. I don't know how I can live. I don't know how I can face tomorrow.


8.6     I think about dying. I wonder how I could die, what I could do to make myself die. But I don't want to die. I just don't want to live. That's silly I say. There must be some way to live with this. There must be something I can do. What? I can't tell anybody. Nobody would believe me.

Nobody believes he hits me. I don't want to be locked up. I don't know how to get away. There is no place for me to go. Not even my Oma in Holland will believe me. This doesn't happen. It doesn't happen to anybody. Maybe I imagined it. If I imagined it why do I hurt so much? I must have deserved it then. How can you deserve it? What did I ever do to deserve this? I think about that. Yesterday when Mom told me to make the beds I played for a long while instead. I always look at the pictures in the books I find under his pillow even though I've been warned not to. I almost told Sister at school what he does to me. I almost told Father in confession what he does to me. This is how god is punishing me.

8.7     Then I hate god too. I don't want anything to do with god if he lets daddy do things to me. I'm sorry, I'm sorry I didn't mean that. Please don't punish me anymore god. I'll talk to mary instead. She'll ask forgiveness for me. I can't take it mother mary, please make it stop. Please ask jesus to make it stop. I'll be good. Please don't let him hit me anymore. Please. I'll be really, really good. I'll pay attention in church. I promise I won't let my thoughts wander in church anymore. I'll say a rosary every day. I'll say two rosaries. I'll say prayers for the souls in purgatory. I'll be so good you won't believe it. I promise. Please, please don't let him hurt me anymore. Please.

8.8     My crying wakes a sister. What's the matter with you? Why are you sitting up? You should go to sleep. It's the middle of the night. I can't sleep. Are you sick? Yes. I'm sick. What's the matter? I don't know. I'm praying. I thought it would help to pray. Nobody listens to me.

Nobody loves me. I feel really sick. Do you want me to get Mom? No? No. You don't understand. If you're sick I should get Mom. No. Don't. I'll be alright. Go back to sleep. I'll just pray for awhile until I feel better.

8.9     I think for a long time. Why is the world this way? Why can he do what he wants? Why can I do nothing I want? Why can he hit me, even when I don't do anything wrong? Why does he like to hurt me? Why can't I live with somebody who would like me? And then it dawns on me. I am not his daughter. I can't be. Nobody treats a daughter like this. I must be adopted. Silly. You're not adopted. I must be. That would explain it. When were you adopted? You remember stuff from when you were little in Holland. It doesn't make sense any other way. Maybe they lied to me. Maybe I really am adopted. Yes. That's it. I'm adopted.

8.10     But that means it won't stop. That means he can do whatever he wants to me. I'm not really his daughter, but he has rights. That means it's never going to stop. I wonder if I could run away. Where could I go? How could I even get out of the house? I look at the window. I could climb on to the porch roof and slide down the tree to the ground. Yes, I could get out. But where would I go? I don't know anybody who would take me. Everybody thinks I am bad because I say bad things about my daddy. They say I don't know what I'm talking about. They say I'm ungrateful. They'd send me home. That would be worse. If I ran away and somebody brought me home he would punish me. And I don't want him to hurt me anymore.

8.11    I have to figure something out. How am I going to live here? I can't stand it anymore. What can I do? There must be something I can do. There's only one thing I can do. Pray. Pray all the time. Every time he hurts you offer up your suffering. That's what the saints did. But I'm not a saint. Yes I am. Don't be silly. You're not a saint. But I am a martyr. This is the kind of suffering martyrs had. No. Martyrs would never have let him do what he did tonight. You let him. You're bad. You better ask forgiveness. On your knees.

8.12    I kneel beside the bed, blanket around my shoulders. I pray to be forgiven my sins. I pray that mother mary will understand why I had to let him do those things to me. I didn't mean to let him. I didn't want to let him. I know I did, but it was so he wouldn't hurt me anymore. I pray to be forgiven, and that she will understand that I don't have the courage of a martyr. I don't like to be hurt. I can't stand it when he hurts me. I am so afraid. I hope she will ask her son to forgive me for being a coward. I don't know if I will go to hell for being a coward. I hope I didn't commit a mortal sin because I couldn't make him stop.

8.13    I lie on the bed. The sky seems lighter. It will be morning soon. Sunday. I will go to church and I will pray like never before. I want to be forgiven for the terrible sin I have committed. I want to be forgiven because I can't love god anymore. I told mother mary that I would never be able to pray to god again. I would pray to her and hope that would be good enough. I still can't sleep. I see her statue on the shelf. The statue Oma gave me for my first communion. I will love you with all my heart I tell her. I need you so much. I need somebody to listen to me. Please.

8.14    I hear the little kids get up. Feet hit the floor and pad downstairs to the bathroom. I turn my face to the wall. I don't want to get up. I don't want to see anybody. I don't want to see him. But it is Sunday. I have to dress for church.

8.15    The walk to church takes forever. I shuffle my feet in the gravel. I can't make myself pick up my feet and walk like a normal person. I hurt everywhere. I don't want anybody to see me. They'll know what I've done. They'll know. If I keep my eyes focussed on my shoes I can make it to church. At church I can pray with my head down. I won't have to look at anybody.

8.16    But nobody notices me. I hear my father talk to somebody after church. They stand on the steps, I am still in the pew. I won't move until he is gone. Everything seems normal. It's only me who is not normal. It's only me. Something is wrong with me. I try to talk to the big statue of mary. I want to light a candle. I think it will help. I know it costs money and I don't have any. I need to light a candle. Nothing is more important. If I can leave that little flame burning, maybe I can convince myself that I am still alive. Maybe it would do what the prayers this morning don't seem to be doing. I take a big risk. There is nobody in the church. I leave the pew and light a blue vigil light on the stand under her statue. I promise to give her the five cents when I have it. I have decided that if anybody catches me I will pretend that I have already put my nickel in the little box or I will pretend I don't know that I need a nickel before I can light a candle. It is so important to leave a lighted candle. I will lie to anybody about it. I don't care what they say. It's a matter of life and death. My life. My death.

8.17    I leave the church and walk home. A sunny spring day. Only it doesn't feel sunny. It doesn't feel right to me that the sun shines at all. I walk to the back gate and look at the house. It looks the same as it did yesterday. The bathroom window is open. I hear my mother calling to one of the kids. I hear the sounds of the table being set for breakfast. The record player plays classical music. My mother tells him to turn the volume down. The same ritual, the same sounds, the same everything as last Sunday and all the other Sundays I remember since I have lived in this house. Why does it feel like a foreign country? What is wrong with me?

8.18    My mother calls my name. I pretend I don't hear her. I have decided that I won't go in until I'm sure they're at the table. Then I will take my place. Then I won't have to talk or look at anyone. She sends somebody to fetch me. I'll be right there. She wants you now. I know, I'll be there in a minute. What's the matter with you? Why won't you answer when she calls you? I'll be right there. Leave me alone.

8.19    Breakfast. What's eating you he says. Nothing. Sit up straight. Where were you? I don't answer. He asks again.

Threat in his voice. Where were you? In church. Doing what? I don't want to answer him. I don't want to look at him. I don't want to tell him about the blue vigil light and mother mary and how they are keeping me alive. Finally I say, praying. And he laughs.

8.20    My mother is outraged. Tries to make him stop laughing. Last night she was not outraged. Why is she outraged now? I know. Last night was only rape. This is sacrilege.

8.21    After breakfast dishes I go back upstairs. I make all the beds and then lie down on mine. Maybe I can sleep. Maybe I can forget. But my head won't quit. It is too dangerous to close my eyes. I see pictures all the time. Pictures of the man with the gold watch chain. I smell his cigar. I smell his breath. My stomach is still upset. I hope I will get sick and die. I hope it happens soon. I don't think I can stand this.

# 9

9.1    *Silence. The Sixth Gate.* Years of silence. Silence wrapped around life like a cocoon. I learn to live in a world where nothing is as it seems. Nothing is as I think it ought to be. Silence. Fear. It is hopeless. A loathing of self without reason. Every year brings more self hate. There is something wrong with me. Everyone tells me. The world is not how you imagine it to be. You've imagined everything. Your pain is imaginary. You are imaginary. You are crazy.

9.2    Life as a void. Life as a black hole in space. All memory, all craziness, stored in a closet at the back of my head. I'll never let it out. I promise. I don't want anybody to know how crazy I really am. I don't want anybody to know how I imagined what happened in the basement. Daddy wasn't any different the next day, his friends were not any different when I next saw them in daylight. I imagined it. Nothing happened. It's me. I'm sick.

9.3    Strange that whatever I remember about my childhood, no matter what it is, my mother says I am wrong. Nothing is as I remember it. I had no childhood. I woke up one morning, forty years old. Nothing had gone before. Several of my sisters had childhoods. They talk to my mother about their memories and she does not tell them they are wrong. Only I am wrong.

9.4     My mother dismisses me. I am not significant. She tells me she does not have a daughter as old as I am. She says that I was always an evil child and I am an obnoxious bitch as a woman. Troublemaker. Liar. Bad, bad girl. There is nothing between us, there never was. Except for my yearning, my four-year-old yearning for my mother. She is not comfortable near me. She has nothing to say to me. She wants nothing from me.


9.5     I search for a mother. Even a memory of a mother who loved me would make me feel less crazy. Years of searching bring me to the woman who could not help me that night in the basement. The woman who walked away because that was the only choice she had. Either watch them rape your eleven-year-old daughter or make coffee. I can forgive that. I have more trouble forgiving her this: she said he told her I liked it and she believed him. Again. She believes still that I was born liking rape. I was born female. I was born a prostitute. Some women were born like that he said.


9.6     Two years ago I told my mother about the violence used against women to force them to have sex. Her mouth tightened. Her body tensed. Is that right? she said in a tone which implied she didn't believe a word. A tone which said: this is another one of your troublemaking lies.


9.7     I have been an orphan most of my life. An orphan. But that's crazy. Another one of your crazy ideas. My sisters talk about their parents and I don't know who they mean. Nobody I know. I don't have any parents. I had a father once. He pimped me to his friends, tried to sell me to

71

one old guy because he wanted me out of his house. Bitch. Obnoxious bitch. How can you say that about your father. The holy father. Daddy, the one who loves you. He really loves you, you know. He said so to me a sister says. Strange. He never said so to me.

9.8     The only time I know he cares is after my littlest sister dies. Then I see him wish me dead. This is what he thinks: I wish to hell it had been you. Nobody gives a damn about you. We all loved her. Why couldn't it have been you, the bitch, instead of the pretty twenty-one-year-old baby who had everything to live for. I see it in his eyes. I have never been wrong about what I see in his eyes. It is never love. It is hate and it is guilt. Never anything else.

9.9     Daddy's greeting to me at thirty-five: get that fucking bitch out of my sight. Daddy's greeting to me at thirty-six when he is drunk: you need a good fuck and daddy's the best man for the job. I always showed you a real good time. You were never grateful. Bitch. Ungrateful bitch.

9.10     Ungrateful bitch. Silent. Stand there and listen to him. Silent. What can I say that would make a difference? Standing before him I am eleven. I am still afraid. I walk away from him. I am silent. He screams after me. You'll be back he says. A party in the back yard of his house, dozens of people, my mother, sisters, in-laws, children. You'll be back for what daddy can give you. They laugh at his joke. Nothing funnier. They think he doesn't mean it. I am silent. I am afraid. I imagined it again. At thirty-six I still imagine such strange things about my daddy. I go home crazy. Again.

9.11     At fifteen I am taken to the doctor by my mother. She complains about my strange behaviour. She fights with her father. She won't co-operate. She won't move or do anything. No. Not anymore. Not since he tried to kill me. Hands around my throat. I'll do the world a favour he says. I'll get rid of this piece of shit. That's what you are. Shit. Garbage. Useless. Crazy. I can't breathe. He won't let me live. I might as well die. I am no longer afraid to die. There is nothing to live for. The doctor decides that I am depressed for no reason. He prescribes Valium.

I can't focus. But I feel better unfocussed. I don't want to live. If I take my pill I don't do anything about dying.

9.12    Everytime I feel the craziness creep up on me I take a pill and the crazy ideas drift into the background.

9.13    I walk through my days as a shadow of myself. I don't want to be myself so it doesn't matter. I walk home from work over the bridge and I think, everyday, that I will jump into the creek below but I don't have the energy to lift myself over the edge. The water dries up in the creek. I'd only hurt myself, I wouldn't drown. Then there's the bus. If I fell in front of the bus would it hurt? Too much. I don't want to hurt anymore. Every day I prepare myself for my last day. I don't have the energy to be creative about dying. I can only think about the bus and the creek. But I don't want my life to end. I just want to get away from home, from my father.

9.14    It is spring. I find a boyfriend at a school dance. Somebody likes me. What does he want? He likes me? Impossible. Nobody likes me. I am not likeable. I don't trust him. The more he likes me the more I don't trust him. The war with my father escalates. I can't go out. I can go out for an hour. I can't go to a dance past nine-thirty. He says I might go and have sex in a car. He won't stand for it. He won't have me giving it away. Giving what away?

# 10

10:1   Dreams. Dreams of a future. A different future than they have all sentenced me to. They all say, my father, the nuns, the priest and my mother, that I will be a breeder, sentenced to provide whatever services the man who owns me demands. All I must do is obey. My father trains me to obey. Obey in silence. Who asked for your opinion? Who said you were supposed to like it? Who told you it would be any different?

10.2   My dreams. Dreams of a life: free. No father, no husband, no man. Free to be who I am. Who am I? Dreams. I am entirely constructed of unlived dreams. Who do I see in those dreams? A woman, strong, healthy, sane and happy. A woman wealthy, powerful and generous. Dreams.

10.3   At first my dreams are small, tentative. I dream only of getting away. Alive. I plot a course for marriage. I know of no other way to leave my father. I am fifteen when I set this plan into action. Eighteen when I am married. Father to husband: she's only ever been used by her father. Husband thought it was a joke. I knew the lie.

10.4　But marriage is not the freedom I dreamt for myself. How could I know I had walked into another sort of trap? He said he'd love me and protect me and take care of me. I believed him.

10.5　Can't you keep this place clean? Can't I have clean shirts and socks? What did I marry you for if you can't even do the basics around here? He said he would help me get away from my father, in return he expected the services of a wife. When I saw what I had done, that I was chained again, I wept. I was lost. There was no hope. Daddy was right. All I had to do was obey in silence and my husband was happy. Never mind, you're not supposed to be happy, you're my wife, doesn't that make you happy enough?

10.6　Different dreams. Dreams of enough wealth so I can live alone. Dreams of a world without male keepers. Dreams of a world where I can live free. But what does that world look like when you are eighteen and terrified? I can not imagine a world in which I can do what I want. The evidence is against it. All women I know are married or about to be married. I know a few widows, but they are married to the memories of their husbands. I know not a single free woman, not a single woman who lives alone because she chooses to. I am assured they do exist.

10.7　I have no skills. I can not make enough money at minimum wage to keep myself in any comfort or even in groceries. I am afraid to be alone. I am afraid to go out by myself, will not go into a restaurant. I know no one. I spend my days taking pills, lying on a bed staring at the ceiling and weeping. Eventually I begin to read all day. I do not cook, I refuse to clean. I do not dress myself.

When my husband comes home from work I put down the book I have been reading and I weep. I cling to him all weekend. You said you'd save me. Why don't you save me then? You're sick he says. Sick. I don't know why I ever bothered to marry you. You're sick and you're useless.

10.8    This is not what I want from my dream. Here take these pills he says. This is life. You can't run away from real life. Why is it real life for me and not for him? Because he's a man and that's the way it works. Then why wasn't I born a man? I want to do the same things he does. Why can't I? You can't even get out of bed. What do you mean you want to do the same things he does? I am asked. I want to have a real life. I want to do something with my life. But of course dear, you can keep his house, you can do his clothes so he always looks good. You can take pride in your home. And you can have his children.

10.9    His children. Don't you want to have my baby? No. What a terrible thing to say. Why not? I don't want to have anybody's baby. I'm not ready to have a baby. I'll never be ready to have a baby. I want a life of my own, I don't want a baby. You're sick, that's what you are he says. It's time to get you fixed up. This has gone on too long. I should have taken you to a shrink before now. I hope they can fix you up. I hope they can stop your crying and snivelling. I'll make the appointment and I'll take you there myself.

10.10   No. Anything but that. Do you think I'm crazy? Oh please don't say you think I'm crazy. Not crazy he says, sick. I'll be good. I'll stop crying, really I will. Only don't make me go to a shrink. Alright. But I want changes around here. I want this place kept spotless. I want my dinner ready when I get home from work. I don't want to have to talk to you about the laundry. I want it done and the ironing too. I'll be good, really I'll be good. And I want to start a baby he says. I think that's what you need. I think that's what will stop your nonsense.


10.11 Nonsense? What about my pain? He says: when you have a baby you won't have time to think about anything but the baby. I don't want a baby. Not now, not ever. Like I said, you're sick. Every woman wants a baby. It's natural. You can't not want a baby, unless you're sick. I'll phone your doctor, he'll suggest somebody. We'll get you fixed up. Then we'll have five kids. I always wanted to have five kids. And you'll be my good little wife and a good little mother. You'll see. The shrink can fix you up so you'll be normal and a good wife and mother.


10.12 I've made the appointment he says. Next Friday we'll go and get you fixed up. I don't want to go. That proves how sick you are. They said you might not co-operate. I'm supposed to call back if you don't co-operate. And then what? They'll give me some pills for you. Different pills than the ones you take now, so you won't be afraid to go to the doctor. They said they could help you. Don't you want to learn to be normal. No. I want the pain to stop. What pain? The doctor says there's nothing wrong with you. Sick people like you always have imaginary pain.

10.13   Dreams of a box. The lid of the box is nailed down over my face. Dreams of a plane crash. My father is dead. My father miraculously alive. My father won't die. Die damn you, die. Don't tell those dreams. Don't say anything about them. They'll say you're crazy. They lock up women like you. The shrink says, do you dream? No. I never dream. I have nightmares. Don't say that. Keep your mouth shut. No, I don't remember what they're about. Why won't you be nice to your husband? Don't you like him? He's okay. He's just not what I want for my life. And what do you want? A real life. My own life. But of course, a wife and a mother, that's real enough for most people. Why isn't it real enough for you? It's not enough. I want to be someone with my life. That's excellent. A good wife and a good mother, the way god made you. No. That's not enough. I don't want that at all. Then why did you marry? To get away from home. Trouble with your mother? No. Trouble with my father. What sort of trouble. I don't know. It must have been with your mother then. No. Well dear I think we'll be able to help you. I want you to take these pills four times a day. I'll talk to your husband to make sure you follow my instructions. I want to see you next Friday. Again? I thought you were supposed to fix me up. Of course dear, but it will take time. You mean I have to come back here? Certainly, is that a problem? But there are crazy people here, I'm not crazy. Of course not dear. See you next Friday.


10.14   Pills. No more tears. Days melt into months. I don't care about anything. I see the shrink on Fridays, the only day I go out. Except Sunday when I go to church. I can't read. My eyes won't focus. The shrink decides I don't like my mother. Tries to talk to me about my mother. I refuse to talk.

He threatens me. If I don't co-operate he will have me locked up for my own good. I make things up for him. He nods in his chair, makes notes on a pad of yellow paper. Time's up, see you next Friday. Here's your prescription. Nothing changes. The new prescription gives me stronger pills. It's so nice to be stoned. I care about nothing. I can even manage to have sex with my husband now, as long as I take a pill half an hour before. He is pleased. He tells the shrink about the progress I have made. They are both pleased.

10.15  The shrink says I am better. As long as I take the pills I will be alright. I will have to take the pills for a long time, maybe always. You can never tell with cases like this. He brings my husband into the office. We will have a conference he says. He describes my progress, that I am as well as I am ever likely to be. His advice is that I should have a baby as soon as possible. She refuses to get pregnant, my husband says. The shrink says he thinks I'll co-operate now and do whatever my husband wants. Because she knows what will happen to her if she doesn't. He looks at me to see that I have understood him. Oh yes. I will be a very good girl. And how am I to make her pregnant if she refuses? Do whatever you have to do, just make her pregnant. It's all she needs. And make certain she takes her pills.

10.16  I manage to talk my husband into postponing the attempts to make me pregnant until after we move. I'd be too sick I explain. I wouldn't want to be puking when there is so much work to be done. I wouldn't be able to do the cleaning or packing. In that case it can be postponed. I try to think of something to further postpone the inevitable. Why am I always trapped? Because you are a woman. It is not a trap, that's just your silliness or your sickness talking. It is a normal woman's life, there's nothing wrong with that, there's just a lot wrong with you. But if there is so much wrong with me it would be dangerous to have a baby. No, he says, he asked the doctor, it wouldn't hurt the baby. What about me? Will it be dangerous for me? Of course not, silly. All normal women have babies. Even when they don't want to?

10.17   In late fall he decides it is time to make me pregnant. He is very organized. He has decided how it will be done. He will have sex with me twice a day every day until I get pregnant. If I don't co-operate he will take me back to the shrink. Meaning if I don't do what he wants he will have me locked up. For my own good. He will come home every-day at noon. I am to have a sandwich ready on the table and I am to be naked on the sofa. He will deposit his sperm, eat his sandwich and go back to work. After supper he will do it again.

10.18   Why is it always like this? Spread your legs. Do as you're told or I'll hurt you. Don't you want to please me? What about me? What about you? he says. Isn't it supposed to be nice for me too? That's not important, the important thing is that you do what you're told. We're trying to help you. Spread your legs. Did you take your pills today? Then why are you crying again?

10.19   Pregnant. Sick. Feeling awful. Why do I have to do this? Why can't I say what I want to do with my life? Why does somebody else always get to decide for me? Won't I ever be free? Free? What's free? Nobody's free to do as they want. Maybe when I retire he says. When's that? Thirty-five years? What about me? Women don't retire. This is your life, there's nothing else. Dreaming about it only makes you sick.

10.20   Dreaming and pregnant. Dreams of escape. Dreams of running. Where, where? Five kids he says. Where can you run with five kids? I don't want any kids. I want a life of my own. Doing what? he asks. I don't know. How many times has he asked me? Always the same answer. I don't know what's possible. I don't know what I want to do. I only know I want something different than this. I don't like sex, I don't like keeping house for him, don't like doing his laundry, cooking his meals. Why am I here at all? Where else can I go? There is no place else to go. I can't go home. I have no money. I have no friends. I have a husband, a keeper to look after me, to make sure I take my pills and eat sometimes. I'm lucky he says, lots of other guys wouldn't put up with me for five minutes.

10.21   Dreams of the box again. The lid nailed down again. Trapped forever. This is the way the world is for women. Fighting it makes me sick. Nobody understands my problem. And then a book understands. Betty Friedan understands. There's somebody else out there. But it's too late. I'm nine months pregnant. Trapped now with a kid on the way. Trapped forever. No hope at all.

10.22   My son is born. Late August. The day after, I wake from the dream of the box again. I have had enough. I will never have another child. I will do something. I will make up my own mind. I will say nothing to anyone. I have decided. Monster. Monster. Yes, monster. But I have decided. I will leave. Leave them both. I don't know where I will go, but I will go. I will not stay to have more children. To die in the box. To smother in a marriage. I will leave. Whatever there is out there can't be any worse than this. I have no hope. I will leave without hope. I will leave with nothing.

# 11

11.1   Bitter. So bitter. No reason to be bitter. You hate men. So unreasonable. Such a bitch. Don't know how to co-operate. Can't say yes. Can't smile. Not sweet. Five foot nothing and vicious. A bitch. No reason at all. What did men ever do to you? Just because you met a bad one doesn't mean they're all like that. They mean my husband. I don't know why I hate all men. I don't mean my ex-husband. I am afraid. No reason. Everything about me is unreasonable.

11.2   Twenty-five and still she has night terrors. Twenty-five and she can't go anywhere by herself. Poor pathetic bitch. She'll never find a man now. Can't smile, can't even be polite. What a fool to leave her husband. What a dangerous bitch. Only a monster mother would leave her child, her son, not yet two years old.

11.3   *The Seventh Gate:* making a career of taking pills with alcohol chasers. She's twenty-seven. No night terrors if you're stoned. Hangovers last all day, every day. It's so easy to get pills, somebody will buy the booze if you hang out in the bar. Looking for a way to throw away the self I don't want. Pick up guys in the bar, throw everything away. Take another pill, another. Don't bother to eat, lots of calories in the booze and a plate of fries in the bar once or twice a week. Even drunk she's a bitch. Nobody wants anything to do with a disaster looking for a place to park.

11.4     Christmas. Working in daddy's store. He takes me out for coffee. Says he notices I'm poor. Says I must not be getting enough to eat. Says he notices my hair is falling out. He has a solution. If I'll co-operate. There are friends of his I could pose for. Nude. They'd pay well and he'd make sure I had lots of money, food. I could pay the rest of my way through school if I was nice to his friends. I don't believe what I hear. I am twenty-seven. I say no. You always were a stupid bitch he says. Always.

11.5     Back to school. Nothing in the books I read for my classes has anything to do with my life. A stupid bitch. A drunk. Stoned all day. Why can't I be reasonable and do what he wants? Why can't I make myself do what he wants? I wouldn't have to struggle so much, wouldn't be so poor. He gave me another chance and I turned him down. Misery. Stupid bitch filled with misery, failing her classes for no reason.

11.6     I see a counsellor. Talk about school. Don't talk about daddy. Talk about lovers. Don't talk about daddy. Try to find a way to stay sober. Don't talk too much. Don't cry. Take pills for distance. Take pills to float your troubles out of sight. Can't read, can't work, can't think. Take more pills. They help for three hours, exactly. Then take another pill. Only one drink. Think I'll see who's at the bar tonight. Come home drunk. Alone. Take a pill so I can sleep, I'm not that drunk, it won't matter. And the next day is the same and the one after that, and the one after that. What's wrong with her? She's bright. Why is she throwing her life away? Stupid bitch can't get her shit together. Not my problem. Hey, save the heavy shit for somebody else, I'm not interested. Drowning. Pills, booze and misery. Drowning.

11.7    Nobody cares. I don't care. Another pill. Another drink. Flush that woman. Nobody cares. Down the nearest sewer. Nobody cares. I don't care.

11.8    I rent a typewriter. It's time to begin writing. I type page after page of numbers. I can't make the words come out. Take another pill. Write a letter then, at least that will make the rental worthwhile. Hi, I'm fine. Having a wonderful time. I love school. I have lots of friends. Lies. Better to type numbers. At least I don't have to admit to the lies behind the numbers. I cry into the machine. I am useless. Like he said. A stupid, useless, rotten bitch. I can't even write a letter. I can't do anything right. I am too stupid to succeed at anything.

11.9    Have a bath. Think of ways to die. Take two pills before the bath. Maybe there will be courage in the pills tonight. Nobody cares. Nobody to talk to. See the kid before you check out. Okay. Not tonight. Won't check out tonight. Try to sleep.

11.10   A weekend with the kid. A stranger. My son. Three years old, trusting. Who are you he asks. I don't know I reply. Why am I here he asks. I don't know. Are you my mommy? I don't know.

11.11 I'm not a mommy. I'm a failure. I fail at everything. I am the only person who has ever managed such remarkable success at failure. I failed my childhood. I failed my marriage. I failed being a mother. I failed school. I even failed suicide. I don't even have the courage to die.

# 12

12.1　My husband never thought I'd leave. He laughs when I tell him. Where will you go? You aren't going to leave me. Yes. Yes. I'll find a place. I'll find a way to leave. Once I know that I am serious I find an apartment in a week. I tell him. He hopes it doesn't have a lease. You'll be back after your little tantrum he says. What will you do for money? I found a job for the summer. In the fall I'll get a student loan and go back to school. You think you've got it figured out eh? You'll be back. But don't wait too long, I might run out of patience. I might not want to take you back. I won't be back. He laughs. You'll be back alright.


12.2　Reading. A new world. Reading women writers: Millet, Greer, Morgan, Lessing, Atwood. Discovery. Beginning again. A journey to self begun at last. Only twenty-five, lots of time. Beginning.


12.3　Division of property: half of the bedding, pots and pans, the cutlery and dishes. My own books. A few records and the stereo. He keeps the television and the washing machine because he keeps the child. Buy a mattress with the first pay. Move everything into a one-room apartment. What did you do for your summer vacation? I am asked in the fall. I left my husband and son. Oh, how interesting.

12.4    My sisters do not understand. How can you leave such a nice man? How can you leave your son? You always were a bitch. Can't love. Never could love anything. You always were a mess. A perfectly good husband and the best marriage you're ever likely to have. No. The only marriage. I tried it once, I didn't like it. Only a fool would do it again. How can you leave that darling baby? What kind of monster are you?


12.5    I stop telling people I have a son. They are too quick with their judgement. Women call me monster, unnatural. No one offers support or understanding. It was beyond reason. My selfishness. You must be crazy. Again.


12.6    No sense that I do the best I can. I know I can't support the child. Know that the hatred growing in me would destroy him. I don't want to destroy him with my pain. And I know I would. Know I cannot help him or myself out of the vortex of hate and pain. So I throw him clear before I am pulled under. And for that I am a selfish monster woman. Not brave. Not wise. A monster.


12.7    No sense of what it costs me to save him. No compassion. You must never ever leave your child. Bad enough to leave your husband, but it happens. People who know find me dangerous, cold-blooded. How many times I see the walls of their fear go up. You should not have left your son. Monster.

12.8   For a year and a half, from four to almost six, I do not see my son at all. I cannot handle more pain than I already have. My world is falling apart. I do not know who he is. I know less who I am. It is better to stay away than to hurt either of us further. He is an ache I cannot soothe, which never leaves me. Guilt: I should be able to keep him. I should be willing to give up school. I should be willing to go on welfare. I should be willing to do anything to keep him. I know his father will not have to leave school or go on welfare to look after him. I know my son will be fed and clothed by his father. I know he will be better off without me. I think the only hope is to get away by myself.


12.9   I find an old church. Sanctuary. A church like the one I ran to as a child. A safe place. No one will find me. No one will hurt me. My own place. A quiet place to go crazy. I think I can fill it with my dreams, hardly notice the lack of walls, or plumbing or cold. Sanctuary. At any price.


12.11   The price is the cold. I would endure poverty anywhere. In the old church it comes with cold. Eventually fibreglass gives me pink walls. A womb structure. A nice soft place to go crazy. Cold. But mine.

12.12   Fill the space with books. Books about religion. Books about women. Books by women. Books about writers. Books about dreamers. Books to bring me real lives. Books to compensate for not having a real life. Books as friends. Books as ships on which I journey. Books as anchors to keep me alive. Books as amulets. A life of books. A better reality. A way to reality. Books instead of life. Safer. Possible.

12.13 A man who is my friend helps make it possible. When I drown in dishes, he rescues. When I drown in despair, he rescues. When I drown in bills and shit, he rescues. Non-resident and still loyal. The best kind of help. He brings chilled Chablis and live lobster because he knows I need it. He brings comfort and support. He doesn't ask me for anything. I almost trust him.

12.14 Learning to live alone. Learning to live. Twice a year I visit an ancient friend. She teaches me about survival, living alone, and poverty with dignity. She is fifty years older than I am. She understands.

12.15 Help arrives too from other women friends. It's amazing you are here at all they say. We will do what we can they say. Produce in the fall, chickens, lamb. Clothing made for me or passed on. Help. Practical help. Phone calls when I have a phone: are you alright? How's it going?

12.16 Going? I wish it was going. The sentence has changed. Once I could not remember. Now I cannot forget.

# 13

13.1   Survival. That's what I want to know about. How do I survive? Pretend he said. Pretend you are somewhere else. Not for him, not to suit his convenience. But I learn to pretend. I learn to dream toward a future where I will be safe. A future of my own making.

13.2   It's a dream. It doesn't matter if you dream big. Big car, big house, big money. It's a dream. Big dreams cost the same as little ones. Might as well dream big.

13.3   Here is my dream: to live alone in a big house in the country. To hear the first meadowlark in spring. To ride my bicycle to the horizon as the sun sets. To read. To paint. To write. My dream. Alone.

13.4   My dream does not include anyone else. I have no energy to bring anyone with me. No energy for relation-ships, not even with a cat or a goldfish. Alone. A dream to stand alone and tall in sunlight. That is enough.

13.5   A gift, finally, from life. Sanctuary. Ten years it takes to learn to live alone, ten years of being crazy with my pain. Ten years which feel like a thousand. Ten years of promising myself each midnight not to die because tomorrow might bring me something better or at least another day to write.


13.6    Survival. Dreaming with a pen in my hand. Writing. Writing. Writing. Who will hear me?

## Epilogue

Light. A crack in the wall of darkness. A single moonbeam of understanding. Waxing. New. Brilliant. White gold promise.

No rescuer. No mother wisdom. Fingernails. Teeth. Determination. Process. Crawl through the mire forever. Toward the mirror. Reflection of scars. Multiplied. Each scar holds a book. Reversed. Read it in the mirror. It is done.

Beginning. Always. From the secret place. Soul dwelling: found. Self: found. Heart: found. Life: found. Wisdom: found. Hope, once lost: found. Process: never lost.

Wandering. Maybe. The path.

Rope ladder. Words in the mirror. Moon. Climb.

Count the stars. Count the words. See the Goddess. In the eyes of a lover.


Woman. Dreaming. The mind. Free. Freedom. Bestowed from within. Self. This night. No longer dark. Star messages. Silver and gold. Blessings. I dream. I love. I am.

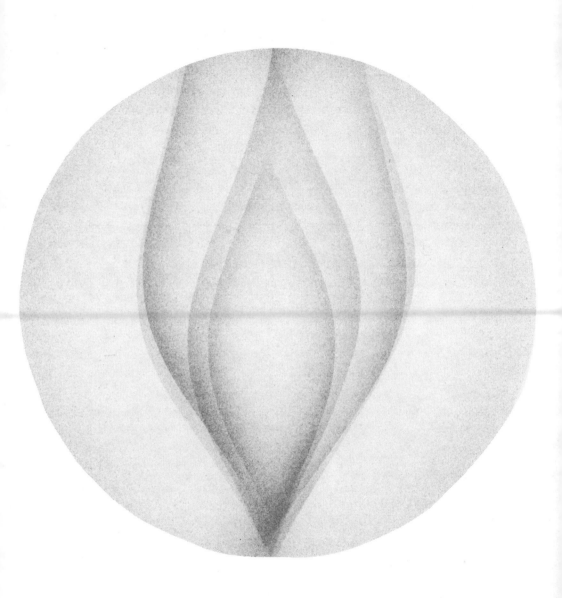

*"Ikon"*, airbrush drawing by Elly Danica, 1988.